THE SEVERN & WYE
RAILWAY

UNIFORM WITH THIS BOOK

AFTERNOON SCENE AT LOWER LYDBROOK

Maid Marian leaving the platform with an up train for Lydney,

THE
SEVERN & WYE
RAILWAY

A History of the Railways of the
Forest of Dean : Part One

by

H. W. PAAR

BASED ON THE WORK OF
'DEAN FORESTER'

DAVID & CHARLES : NEWTON ABBOT

'This was a wonderful thicke Forest, and in former ages so darke and terrible, by reason of crooked and winding ways, as also the grisly shade therein, that it made the inhabitants more fierce, and bolder to commit robberies, for in the reign of Henry VI, they so infested all Severn Side with robbing and spoiling that there were lawes made by Parliament for to restrain them. But since that rich mines of iron were here found out those thicke woods began to wax thin by little and little.'

—William Camden, BRITANNIA, circa 1585.

ISBN 0 7153 5707 7

First Published 1963
Second Edition 1973

Set in 10 on 11 point Pilgrim
and Printed in Great Britain
by Redwood Press Limited Trowbridge
for David & Charles (Holdings) Limited
South Devon House Newton Abbot Devon

Contents

Illustrations

between pages 80 and 81

between pages 96 and 97

between pages 112 and 113

between pages 128 and 129

IN TEXT

These symbols are used in maps throughout the book

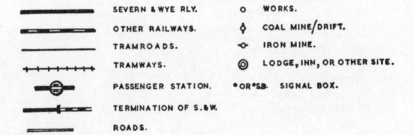

SEVERN & WYE RLY.	o WORKS.
OTHER RAILWAYS.	◊ COAL MINE/DRIFT.
TRAMROADS.	⦦ IRON MINE.
TRAMWAYS.	◎ LODGE, INN, OR OTHER SITE.
PASSENGER STATION.	•OR•SB. SIGNAL BOX.
TERMINATION OF S.&W.	
ROADS.	

Notes

THE RAILWAYS

The following summary will establish the broad outlines of Forest railway development, as the history of the Severn & Wye system is bound up with that of its neighbours, the subject of a companion volume, *The Great Western Railway in Dean.*

In the period 1809—1815 three tramroads were established: *The Severn & Wye Railway & Canal Company* built a line linking the two rivers, with branches, serving the western valley. Locomotives were introduced in 1864, a temporary broad-gauge railway was laid up to Mierystock in 1868, and in 1869 a policy of extension and conversion was begun on standard gauge. In 1879 the company amalgamated with the Severn Bridge Railway, the s & w & sbr was taken over jointly by the GWR and MR in 1894, and the line is now part of the Western Region of British Railways.

The Bullo Pill Railway Company served the eastern valley from the Cinderford area to the Severn. It was taken over by the South Wales Railway, and a broad-gauge line (the Forest of Dean branch) was completed in 1854, being converted to standard gauge in 1872.

The Monmouth Railway Company linked Monmouth with Coleford and the Forest, having one short-lived connection with the s & w. The Coleford, Monmouth, Usk & Pontypool Railway Company purchased the Coleford to Monmouth section in 1853, but failed to convert it into a railway, this being done by the Coleford Railway in 1883.

The three tramroads did not compete to any great degree, but in 1826 there was an abortive proposal to build the Purton Steam Carriage Road, between the s & w and the Forest of Dean lines. Eventually the *Forest of Dean Central Railway* was built, from New Fancy colliery down to Awre on the South Wales line, but it was ill-fated.

The Mitcheldean Road & Forest of Dean Junction Railway, promoted in 1871 to carry the Forest of Dean branch northward to the Hereford, Ross & Gloucester Railway, was completed after difficulties, and purchased by the GWR, but was only opened as far as Drybrook.

TERMS

Tramroad. A track composed of L-type tram-plates, for the passage of horse-drawn wagons with flangeless wheels. In their earliest days, in the Forest, such lines were generally termed 'railways', 'rail roads' or 'railroads'; later they were generally referred to as 'tramways'.

Tramway. A narrow-gauge railway, worked by horse, rope or locomotive power. Such lines were sometimes described as 'trolley roads' in the latter half of the 19th century.

Licence. Industrial activities in the Forest were carried on under licence from the Surveyor General of His Majesty's Land Revenue. An Act of 1812 empowered his successors, the Commissioners of Woods, Forests & Land Revenues (under Treasury authority), to grant leases for tramroads for periods up to 31 years, provided that there was no interference with the rights of the Bullo Pill or s & w companies. Nearly all the private branch lines were built under such licences.

Free Miners. The mining rights were Crown property, but at a remote date the Free Miners were granted special privileges (see *The Free Miners*, by C. E. Hart, 1953). Briefly, they had the right to acquire conditionally exclusive grants to win minerals in the Forest, paying only a royalty therefor, the grant of free timber for mining purposes, and the right to try cases affecting the mines in their own Mine Law Court.

CHAPTER 1

Before the Platelayers Came (1799-1809)

THE FOREST

The great Forest was never simply a woodland, for the district was rich in minerals, particularly coal and iron. The Romans built several roads, which decayed after them, transport reverting to pack mules on primitive tracks. The magnitude of the mineral wealth is indicated by the fact that in medieval times the Forest was the major iron-working centre in Britain, and although subsequently the industry was hampered by its reliance on charcoal fuel, which conflicted with the Crown's interest in preserving the timber, the works were rehabilitated with the introduction of coke smelting in the latter years of the 18th century.

It was upon the sure foundation of mineral wealth, and its need for effective transport, that the horse tramroads were to be established; these now pleasant byways were vital outlets for a multitude of enterprises. The tramroads were notably versatile, being quickly and cheaply constructed on the contours of the land, with few bridges, tunnels or heavy earthworks; but their operation was leisurely, limited by the pace and sinews of the motive power, and they were soon faced with the prospect of the steam railway, either as successor or competitor.

POOR ROADS AND DEAR COAL

Between 1761 and 1786 over £11,000 was spent by the Crown in road improvements, but mostly on the roads east from Coleford, which had little value as mineral outlets to the rivers, being travellers' roads from Gloucester to South Wales. Yet the deputy surveyor of the Forest (chiefly concerned with timber conservation) deprecated the expense as encouraging the use of wheeled vehicles for coal transport, thus leading to the taking of more pit timber.

In the closing years of the 18th century the roads were impassable in winter, and always dangerous, the coal wagons requiring large teams of horses. Some £10,600 was spent on repairs, but again the accent was mainly on the travelling public—'post chaises at 1s per mile, and sober drivers', advertised one innkeeper, announcing a new road. Little maintenance was undertaken in the next 30 years, and bad roads were advanced as a reason for building churches and schools in the Forest, those outside being inaccessible. A canal was proposed, but without much enthusiasm.

Such conditions kept the price of coal at a high level in surrounding markets, with repercussions on the pits themselves—in August 1787, of 121 pits, 31 were not working, and under 2,000 tons of coal were produced per week by the remainder.[1] The pits were worked by free miners, but soon capitalists were appearing as large-scale employers of labour and machinery, and the iron works, moribund for years, were being rebuilt, requiring ore and limestone in quantity. In the closing years of the 18th century the price of coal at Hereford was often as high as £1 15s a ton, and subscriptions were raised nearly every winter to supply the poor.[2] Many meetings were held, and at one of them, in 1799, it was resolved that railways from the collieries to the Wye and Severn would be highly advantageous to Hereford and Gloucester. Years later, in 1835, Thomas Phillips piously informed the Dean Forest Commissioners: 'The railroad was first proposed and for many years perseveringly pressed upon the Crown from the purest motives of benevolence, to raise the Foresters from a state . . . nearly as wretched as anything now existing in Ireland'.

The promoters approached the Bristol Corporation for support. The last Custom Duty Act, however, had, by omitting the words 'by sea' in the schedule for coal after 'port to port', tacitly applied the duty to coal sent from the port of Gloucester to the port of Bristol, and Richard Bright of Bristol had to reply, 'I am sorry to say that your coal is liable to the coast tax and we cannot have it brought here'.[3] Meetings took place in 1799—1800 between Colonel Scudamore (MP for Hereford City), gentlemen of Gloucester and Herefordshire and the Verderers of the Forest, who at that time approved of the measure.

THE FIRST SURVEY

A committee was formed, and at the Swan Inn, Ross, on 22 September 1801, it received a survey prepared by Henry Price of Hereford, and a report by Benjamin Outram.[4] Although the report envisaged a line linking the Severn and the Wye, it was decided to make separate applications to Parliament for two unconnected lines, one to Lydbrook, the other to Lydney, as the Gloucester promoters, hit by the failure of the Gloucester & Berkeley Canal, decided not to unite with those from Hereford.

Petitions were presented in January 1802 for leave to bring in bills, and the Treasury was asked for Crown consent. It referred the matter to the Surveyor General of His Majesty's Woods; he consulted the Lord Warden, Verderers, and Forest officers, who all expressed strong opposition, as did the turnpike trustees. The objections, largely the result of Teague & Co.'s activities in opening a coal mine, and building a tramroad thence to the Wye at Lydbrook, in defiance of the Crown officers[5], were briefly as follows.[6]

Powers were sought to make branches to any workings within three miles of the main lines—the Forest could be cut into a 'gridiron'; the earthworks would obstruct the hauling of Navy timber along traditional routes, and the Crown would lose control of large areas of the Forest; 'foreign' capitalists would expand the coal industry at the expense of the woodlands, and acquire the rights of the free miners; thus the old locally-owned collieries would be ruined and a monopoly interest left in charge of both railway and industry; the lessening of traffic on the turnpike roads, rendering the tolls insufficient to maintain them. Memorials supporting the schemes were, however, sent by free miners and inhabitants of Hereford and Monmouth.

The northern line, surveyed by Price in 1801, was to have been some 3¼ miles long, from a summit south-east of Mierystock Bridge to an inclined plane at Lydbrook. The Parliamentary proceedings were short and unsuccessful, for full newspaper notice had not been given, nor all land-owners notified. Price's route for the southern scheme is again similar to that later adopted, from Lydney Pill serving Parkend and terminating near York Lodge. This measure was reported upon, and a bill ordered, but not presented; possibly the promoters were apprehensive because again adequate newspaper notice had not been given.[7]

Price, a non-partisan, also prepared a plan of the two schemes, to accompany the very adverse 'Report on the intended railroads' sent by Thomas Blunt, the deputy surveyor, to John Robinson, the Surveyor General[8], and in 1802 he surveyed a line from the opposite bank of the Wye near Lydbrook to Hereford which, however, never reached Parliament.[9]

Outram's report[10], dated 5 September 1801, noted that the two western valleys suited a line linking the rivers. The northern collieries were favourably situated for supplying the Wye valley, and a branch could be made along Serridge Hill to pits which would serve for many years, after which other lines could be constructed to deeper works on the south side of Serridge.

Northward from the summit he envisaged a gradient of 1 in 66 and at the Wye a self-acting incline about 180 yd long with nearly 150 ft fall, as a line along the bottom of the valley would be too steep, and crowded by the road and works. Outram urged the improvement of the Wye, to increase the agricultural use of lime by cheap transport, in conjunction with the tramroads.

South from Serridge, the route was by Parkend furnace to wharves at Jack's Pill, near Lydney. Outram, who had taken a second opinion from Hodgkinson[11], estimated the cost at £21,500 for the main line from Lydbrook to Jack's Pill, 13¾ miles.

After the failure of the two schemes, there was an abortive proposal, under the auspices of the Hereford promoters, to secure powers for the complete line, with the intention of building only the sections at each end; they were particularly anxious to secure the line to the Wye, as they were planning one thence to Hereford.[12]

In 1804 an approach was made for the complete line, with three branches specified to meet previous objections, but the Forest officials repeated all their previous objections to the Surveyor General, Lord Glenbirvie, adding that Lydney Pill was an unsuitable terminus. Glenbirvie reported adversely and Charles Bathurst, a prominent landowner at Lydney, thought further attempts useless while he continued in office.[13]

It was in February 1804 that Trevithick's pioneer railway locomotive started working on the Penydarren tramroad.

RENNIE'S REPORT

Lord Robert Spencer, appointed Surveyor General in 1806, favoured railways, and Lord Grenville, First Lord of the Treasury, expressed some intention of the Government making them. Spencer visited the Forest, and was chiefly concerned about the taking of timber under ancient custom: 'something must be arranged to induce miners to give up their timber'.[14] This was of vital importance for ship-building, with the French war being conducted largely at sea—indeed, Nelson himself had visited the Forest in 1802.

Glenbirvie had referred the question of railways to John Rennie,

TRAMROADS IN ACTION

(1) *Bicslade branch. A burst of speed past Cannop Ponds, 1943*
(2) *Wimberry Slade, about 1933. End-tipping coal wagon*

TRAMROAD ENGINEERING

(3) *The Bishopswood branch, high above the Wye, with Lydbrook viaduct beyond*

(4) *Wimberry Slade, 1935. Hopewell High Level pit. Note braking 'sprags' and shoes*

(5) *Wimberry Slade, 1935. Details of a 'turnout'*

(6) *Lower Lydbrook, 1952. Tramroad formation above Lydbrook viaduct. The incline head is to the right of the garage*

the eminent civil engineer, before resigning, but before Rennie could report, notice was given on 12 September 1806 of an application for a railway from Lydbrook to Lydney Pill, Nass Point and Purton, with branches.

Grenville dropped his own idea, and Spencer proposed that both Eastern[15] and Western lines be built by subscribers—he would not recommend one alone, because the colliers would expect both, to induce them to give up their claims to timber, and it appeared impracticable to build a branch from Cinderford Bridge to Parkend.

Rennie's report[16], of great interest because he undertook very little railway work, was embodied in a letter to Spencer dated 12 February 1807. Rennie anticipated little traffic into the Forest (some corn, cider, apples, etc., during droughts when the Wye could not be navigated) and recommended a general gradient of about 1 in 143, on which a horse would pull downwards some 12 loaded wagons taking about $1\frac{1}{2}$ tons each, returning with the same number empty.

Rennie favoured a harbour at Nass Point, with a basin, as the sandy river bed would not make a good anchorage. Having the basin close to the Severn and the railway down to it would save about £2,500, or a canal could be made to Lydney. The canal would not have enough water from the inland streams, and the Severn would bring much silt, so he proposed a short cut from the iron mills to convey their tail water to the canal.

The Lydbrook incline was to be 238 ft high instead of 150 ft, thus easing the gradient from Mierystock Bridge to 1 in 132. From the head of this valley his line crossed the road by a cutting, then descended at 40 ft to the mile along the east side of the valley to Parkend furnace and Lydney.

Branches were recommended along Serridge Summit, from Parkend to Moseley Green (and eventually to Foxes Bridge), from Parkend *via* an incline to Nags Head pits, with possible extension to Coleford and Monmouth, and another to stone quarries near Cannop Bridge, *via* a plane worked by a small steam engine, 'a trivial expense'. The trade would be principally to Bristol, and coal duty would be almost prohibitive, but he thought it could be waived by the Act, as in the case of the Monmouthshire Canal.

Rennie divided the area into 'eastern and western spheres of influence', his line from Blakeney to Danby Lodge, and thence a little west of Churchway Engine being cited for many years in opposing measures for new lines. He thought that forfeit of timber rights would be compensated by the advantages of railways. He

B

estimated that a single track from Lydbrook to Lydney, the canal and harbour, and Lydbrook incline would cost just under £40,000, and branches some £12,000.

In March 1807 a petition for a modified line, from Lydbrook to Newerne with branches and a canal, was referred to a Commons committee which included Sir George Cornewall (MP for Hereford County and a subscriber); Rennie informed it that the line was 'irregular and of uncertain declination and by no means capable of affording that great saving of labour which it is the object of a Railway to effect'. The committee reported that Rennie's own line was on better gradients and would not involve any further land-owners, but proceedings ceased.

A HARD BARGAIN

A new factor now entered the politics of Forest railway promo-tion. An Act of 1808 re-affirmed an old power of the Crown to enclose up to 11,000 acres of the Forest, and Commissioners were appointed to lay out the plantations. Headed by Glenbirvie as Surveyor General (he had resumed office in 1807) they included many who supported the railway schemes. Glenbirvie was keen to start re-afforestation, for which he required a steady income, and Spencer had suggested that the railways should provide an annual Crown rental of £300. Glenbirvie increased this to £400 (£230, Severn & Wye line, £100, Bullo Pill line, and £70, Monmouth line), according to Thomas Phillips, and he also insisted that the lines should be fenced, 'no more than the most generous landowner would ask'. Afterwards it appeared that this meant the companies should pay for the whole length, and not necessarily along the lines but round the plantations, which Glenbirvie apparently admitted could not have been planted but for the railways. He also increased the rent of the s & w from £230 to £300 until the Mon-mouth Railway should be sanctioned[17], but when this happened the s & w figure was not adjusted.[18]

After many meetings, the free miners were persuaded to 'give up their obnoxious rights' (of cutting timber), the proprietors of collieries near the Severn agreed to pay the same tonnage as the most distant, and the owners of the best coal agreed to pay double the rate charged for the inferior, thereby putting 'all miners upon an equality'.[19]

In 1808, yet another survey was prepared[20], by Astley Bowdler, ready for the next Session. His estimate was as follows:

Single iron railway with passing places, inclined plane at 'Lidbrook', double road near Cross Pills, bridges, culverts, embankments, and land purchase £15,740

A 'tunnell' and deep cutting through the hills from Miery-stock to the west end of Serridge Hill, 713 yd £1,426

A cutting near Pool Dam at Upper Forge £100

Machine ropes, etc. on inclined plane, weighing machines, etc. £650

Branches immediately wanted to Churchway, up Howler Slade and to the Birches, 4 miles 25 chains £4,882

Contingencies £2,500

Total   £25,298

A further £9,250 was estimated for 'remaining branches not immediately wanted, 7 miles 69 chains'.

The Lydney & Lidbrook (sic) Railway Act, 49 Geo III c. 159, received the Royal Assent on 10 June 1809, although no power was given for making the canal.

CHAPTER 2

The System Takes Shape (1809-1840)

PARLIAMENTARY POWERS

The Act authorised the construction and maintenance of a 'Railway or Tram Road' from Lydbrook to Lower Forge *via* Mierystock and Parkend*, with eight branches, from Kidnall's Mill to Phelps Meadows, *via* Moseley Green, from Parkend Bridge to the Birches*, from near Parkend Bridge to Milkwall, up Brookhall Ditches, to Bixhead Quarries, up Howlers Slade*, up Wimberry Slade, and from Mierystock to the summit at Churchway Engine.* Three years were allowed for completing the lines marked *, but no time limit was specified for the others.

Some 55 subscribers were incorporated as the Lydney and Lidbrook Railway Company; they included David Mushet, the Protheroes (Edward, John and Philip) and Samuel Hewlett, local industrialists whose names will recur later. The capital authorised was £35,000, the bulk in £50 shares, but £3,000 in £10 non-voting shares was reserved until 1 August for the free miners, and a further £20,000 was authorised if necessary, as a capital issue or on mortgage.

The company's clerk was to deliver to the deputy surveyor each Monday morning the names of free miners and carriers using the tramroads, for the Act forbade such use by miners claiming free timber, or opening unauthorised workings more than 100 yd from the line (Peter Teague told the Dean Forest Commissioners in 1835, 'by using the Railroad I have given up my right to timber'). Gates were to be erected by the company to give passage to landowners and to prevent cattle straying, and a drawbridge or swivel-bridge was authorised over Pidcock's canal, near Lydney (see Chapter 12).

The Surveyor General and the Navy Board were authorised to make branches, and to carry timber at a reasonable payment, but there is no evidence that any Crown branches were laid. Payments to the Crown comprised one guinea per week towards the cost of inspectors and £300 p.a. rent for land used. Reduced maximum rates were fixed for coal won by certain of Bathurst's tenants, if sent to their forges near Lydney. Bathurst was to allot land for public wharves near Lower Forge, to be guaranteed by the company to give him an annual income of at least £500. Lords of Manors and landowners were authorised to erect wharves, cranes and warehouses and levy charges for their use, but if they refused, the company could erect them, after 12 months' notice. Commissioners were appointed to settle differences between the company and landowners.

THE SEVERN & WYE RAILWAY & CANAL COMPANY

A further Act, of 21 June 1810[1], changed the name of the undertaking to that above, and authorised a deviation (already carried out) from the east side of Upper and Middle Forge pools to the west side, a 500-yd deviation near Daniel Moor Ditches, an extension from Lower Forge, branching along each side of Lydney Pill to Cross Pill, an extension from Lydbrook to Bishopswood, and the canal and harbour at Lydney. Bathurst's tenants (principally John Pidcock & Homfray, of Lydney Forges) could use the waterways gratis and, if not usable, the tramroads beside them, for conveying materials to and from their works—hitherto, of course, they had enjoyed free access to the Severn *via* Lydney Pill.

The first general meeting was held at the King's Head Inn, Ross, on 22 June 1809, and a committee of management was appointed. This met as needed, sometimes several times a month, and became 'the board' in 1853. Its first meeting was on 3 July 1809, at the Plume of Feathers Inn, Lydney, often used thenceforward; the early meetings were presided over by John Protheroe, quickly succeeded by Edward Protheroe. Later the company established its head office at Severn House, Lydney, and the engineer's office was at the nearby Foundry House.

BUILDING THE TRAMROAD

Contracts were awarded in August 1809 to James Barnes for the Parkend—Lydney section, and Edward Moss (or Morse) for Churchway to Lydbrook, and it was decided to shorten Lydbrook incline by increasing the gradient from the Forest. In October, David Morgan undertook the Serridge Summit cutting at 1s 3d per cubic yd. Barnes and Morgan were given the contracts for the rest of the main line and time-limited branches at 5s 9d per yd single track and 9s 7d per yd double track (exclusive of the Summit cutting, 'filling the valley at Mierystock Bridge', and of the track itself), to be completed by 4 August 1810.

In January 1810[2] timber 'cut on the Rail Road from Miery Stock to Lidbrook' was being auctioned by order of the Surveyor General, and in May, timber cut between Cannop Bridge and Parkend. An announcement of the sale of Lydney Ironworks, dated 21 May[3], referred to 'a railway just finished to the River Severn'. Traffic on the tramroad appears to have started in early June, for an advertisement of 4 June 1810[4] stated that Low Delph coal would be sold at 'the wharf of the railway at Lydney, upon the Turnpike Road, at 11s per ton'. On 10 July it was ordered that 'no more carriage of goods be permitted on the Rail Road until the weighing machine is set up', so apparently there had been a rush to take advantage of the new, and for the moment virtually free, transport. On 16 October Barnes reported 'the double road from Parkend, except where the single road is made at the tail of the Pool . . . will be completed in the course of the present week'. It was agreed to economise by making the line in Mierystock cutting single track for 190 yd.

This haste was unfortunately at the expense of good workmanship, for in July 1810 'great defects' existed in Barnes's work, and further examples soon came to light; in December the committee, finding the drawbridge over Pidcock's canal made of beech, required Barnes to replace it with oak. In August 1810 gates were being put up on the 'railroad' above Lydbrook, but difficulty was being experienced with Mierystock cutting. In February 1811 Barnes stopped work, and a serious dispute arose, the company alleging poor workmanship and failure to meet contract time; Barnes claimed that his work was sound, and that the company was not supplying sufficient rails, and owed him money. Roger Hopkins (the acting engineer—see later) arranged for the completion of the line from Parkend to Bixhead Slade, with the Bicslade branch, and by July the dispute had been settled in favour of the company. Early in 1811 part of 'the double road' from Parkend to Lydney had to be relaid, striking evidence again of bad workmanship.

FINANCIAL TROUBLE—AND DIVIDED INTERESTS

A third Act, of 26 June 1811[5], confirmed the power to build the Bishopswood Extension, permitted certain harbour tolls to be levied and authorised an increase in capital of £30,000, the original capital and most of the additional £20,000 having been spent. Money was not readily come by, and the company issued a leaflet dated 24 September 1811[6], which stated that about 22 miles of 'rail road' were complete, and the rest progressing; it was anticipated that the canal and lock, to take vessels of 200 tons burthen, would be complete in November, and the whole undertaking in June 1812.

The traffic anticipated was coal and stone to the Wye for Hereford, Ross, etc., which then totalled some 100 tons per day, most of which it was hoped would come to the tramroad. Traffic from the Wye was expected to be bark, timber and corn from Hereford and Shropshire, to be enticed across the Forest to avoid the 'tedious navigation of the Wye', particularly in summer. Lydney was expected to handle 300 tons of coal and 100 tons of stone per day.

The leaflet quoted the following figures:

				Tons per annum
Expended	£46,417		*Anticipated Traffic*	
Engagements to Bankers, Founders for iron rails, for land, etc.	£11,913		Coal and stone, Lidbrook line, to Wye	30,000
Wanted to complete works	£16,870		Corn, bark, timber from Wye	10,000
			Coal and stone to Lydney	120,000
TOTAL	£75,200		TOTAL	160,000

At 2s per ton for the whole distance on stone and good coal (100,000 tons) and 1s per ton for inferior coal (60,000 tons) an annual return of some £13,000 was expected, with the possibility of putting the tolls up to 3s and 1s 6d respectively later.

Each year there were to be found £352 10s for Crown Rent and Inspectors, £150 for Roynon Jones, in lieu of lockage on the Nass Estate, and £500 for Bathurst's guaranteed wharfage. The latter, it was hoped, would be produced by letting the wharves, and the others from receipts for upwards traffic from Lydney not assessed.

Friction within the ranks of the proprietors is revealed by a circular of 5 March 1812[7], prepared by David Mushet, one of the committee, in answer to that of two proprietors, Atherton and Whitworth. Mushet stated that the company had early decided to complete all the main line and branches (28 miles in all), but the harbour, when begun, drew money away and slowed up progress; the company had raised only £3,000 by the 1811 Act.

Atherton and Whitworth, Mushet said, had collieries on the

Howlers and Birches branches, and had forced through a resolution giving these preference over all other works. Mushet pointed out that no coal was likely to originate on either, for about 18 months, but the harbour was necessary for the company's prosperity—'if the lower works are given up for only one month Lydney will not be a harbour for another season'. The 'opposition' had made much of the fact that branches had been completed to Protheroe's and Mushet's works, but Protheroe had on hand at least 1,000 tons of coal 'got for the purpose of the rail road trade', while on the other line some 1,000 tons of coal and stone were carried in the first three months, and it served another mine and nearly 20 quarries.

Bowdler was—*sub rosa*—looking after the interests of a group of the proprietors ('the Wilts & Berks interest', as Mushet termed them), by pushing forward the Milkwall branch, not merely as their agent, but as manager of, and partner in, some large undertakings *en route*—at a time when the company considered him as exclusively in its employment. These shareholders in the Wilts & Berks Canal, opened in 1810, had subscribed to the S & W to secure a source of coal alternative to the Somerset field. They included William Whitworth, the former engineer of the W & B Canal, and Joseph Priestley, probably he who published *An Historical Account of the Navigable Rivers, Canals & Railways of Great Britain* in 1831.

Mushet suggested that Atherton and Whitworth wanted to hold up shipping of coal at Lydney until their collieries were ready for the market. Nevertheless, Bowdler's estimate had included a sum 'to branches immediately wanted to Churchway, up Howler Slade, and to the Birches', and these were given a time limit; as late as March 1812 it was resolved that the main line and these branches should be completed before 10 June, when the powers would lapse, and the harbour, as Mushet foresaw, was not completed until 1813.

MORE FINANCIAL TROUBLE

On Tuesday, 16 March 1813, a special meeting at the Feathers Inn resolved to circularise the shareholders thus: 'The water was let into the canal and basin this day[8], and the railways being in a state of work, the undertaking may therefore be considered as complete . . . a considerable debt has been incurred, to liquidate which, the sum of £10,000 must be immediately raised.' In April, Hill & Hopkins were suing the company for nearly £7,000, owing for tramplates. A fourth Act was secured on 18 May 1814[9], permitting an increase of capital by £30,000.

The years-old struggle between England and France was slowly being resolved, culminating at Waterloo on 18 June 1815; in October a dividend of 30s per share, amounting to £5,643, was paid. In April 1819, however, the half-yearly dividend was only 12s and by October 1822 it had shrunk to 7s, explained as the result of the increased value of money from the resumption of cash payments; the mine-owners had to reduce wages, provoking strikes and riots. As early as May 1816 men employed on the tramroad had been given a month's notice that their wages would be lowered to 15s a week (in 1854 wages were increased from 2s 8d to 3s per day).

The original Act authorised the company to accept a lump sum for the right to collect and retain the tolls. The company would thus have had a fixed income while the lessee would make a profit if traffic was good. In 1822 the Park End Coal Co., John Trotter & Co., David Mushet and another proposed to lease their own rates; these four alone would have provided a guaranteed annual income of £6,750, but Mr Sugden, the solicitor for the original Act, advised that the plan was illegal, and the traders relinquished their claim.

THE THREAT OF COMPETITION

The company had some competition from the roads, particularly between Churchway and Lydbrook, and also had to look to competition from other industrial districts in its markets. In January 1815 Sheasby was instructed to go to the 'Abergavenny Railroad' (the Llanvihangel Railway)[10], find the price of coal being delivered at the terminus, and estimate the price at Hereford, if it was extended there. (When it was, in 1829, S & W coal traffic to Bishopswood was hard hit, and a rebate on tolls failed to revive it, Forest coal at Hereford costing 20s 6d per ton.) In March 1815 the Oxford Canal Co. was objecting to Dean coal being supplied in Oxford, and the committee considered establishing a public wharf in the town, to receive coal from Lydney only, but no such far-flung outpost was set up. In 1825 the company supported a scheme for a railway to Ross and Wilton, but declined its construction and management.

The Purton Pill Steam Carriage Road scheme was announced to the committee by Sheasby in October 1826; a sub-committee was formed to watch the interloper, and liaison was even effected with the Forest of Dean Railway. A meeting of free miners at Yorkley on 5 March 1832[11] revealed strong feelings about Forest railway monopoly; the resolutions ascribed the whole of the distress of the district to the monopoly of a few individuals, stated that coal carried on the tramroads cost 14s per ton at Bullo Pill and Lydney, that the Forest could only secure a trade for a few months of the year as coal from other districts was sold in their markets at less than 10s per ton, and that it was vain for the proprietors to contend that existing lines were adequate, or that suitable branches could be made, as they could not even convey the traffic they had, except at enormous cost. The Forest was then turbulent, and in 1831 land and mine disputes culminated in riots, destruction of enclosure fences and the calling out of troops.

The company paid out some £350 p.a. in salaries in the 1830s, and assisted local institutions by donations (in 1852, £25 was subscribed to the re-pewing of Lydney Church on condition that 'a pew in a good situation is appropriated to the use of the Company's agent'). Between 1830 and 1833 some £500-£600 p.a. was spent on tramroad repairs, rising to about £1,000 by the 1840s. In the half-year 1838-1839 the accounts were balanced at £6,390 15s 5d, £4,594 5s 0d being carried down.

In 1839 the FODR proposed a branch from Cinderford Bridge to a new harbour at Brimspill, and the S & W opposed it.[12] Lydney and Bullo Pill were already too small, and it is not surprising that both companies were seeking a fresh harbour. These difficulties were largely resolved some years later by the South Wales Railway, which led much of the coal away overland. The S & W proposed the 'Severn & Wye Branch Railway', to run south-west from Lydney Church to a new harbour at Grange Pill for vessels too large for Lydney. Thomas Fulljames, a civil engineer, surveyed Grange Pill, but the scheme was ill-supported and was not developed, although plans were deposited in 1840.

PERSONALITIES

The first clerk was Charles Phillips, also a subscriber. Astley Bowdler, appointed clerk and engineer in June 1809 at £210 p.a., had prepared the plans whilst living at Edenwall House, near Coleford. He was assisted by Barnes (later one of the contractors) and 'there being no public house at Parkend then' they stayed at Whitemead Farm, held by John Teague. His young son, William Teague, helped them by holding the surveyor's chain, later worked among the navvies, and in 1875, aged 81 years, jokingly claimed to be the 'oldest S & W servant'.[13]

After a year Bowdler found that he could not attend to both his duties, so was retained as engineer only at £100 p.a., while Morgan

Parry, erstwhile clerk to the Monmouthshire Canal Company, was appointed clerk and manager in July 1810 at 200 guineas.

Bowdler's reputation soon sank considerably, for he was partial to the Wilts & Berks interest, and later refused to supervise work at the harbour, for in July 1810 the committee modified his specification by shortening the basin, making the slopes 'as steep as they will stand' (to be walled later if necessary), and reducing the canal to single-vessel width, putting in two passing places. On 30 August the company, greatly dissatisfied, discharged him.

Josias Jessop[14] was engineer for a short time. He had assisted his father William on the Croydon, Merstham & Godstone Railway. In October 1810 his proposal to modify the basin was accepted, and it was also decided to abandon the outer harbour *pro tem.* Jessop seems to have done little, for in December the committee asked Mushet to find a superintendent for the work at Mierystock cutting, and for 'putting the present road in complete repair', and in January 1811 the Monmouth Railway 'politely consented to spare Mr Hopkins their engineer'.

Thomas Sheasby[15] with engineering experience on the Swansea (c 1795) and Aberdare (1810) Canals, was an arbitrator for the company in February 1811, in the dispute with Barnes, when he was described as a coal merchant of Swansea. He soon impressed the committee, who were dissatisfied with Jessop and wanted a combined engineer, manager and clerk, Parry being purely an accountant. On 3 July Jessop departed and Sheasby became clerk and superintendent of works.

The committee settled most matters concerning traffic, improvements, etc., advised by their clerk. Sheasby was thus manager, secretary, engineer, and faithful watch-dog over the company's affairs. He brought an almost Pepysian energy and efficiency to his work, checking tonnage, supervising new works, and waylaying offenders, and his zeal made him enemies, as in 1837, when his investigation of wagon overloading brought him an anonymous letter and broken windows. Protheroe's letter of December 1840 (see Chapter 5) reflects much resentment of Sheasby, yet the company recognised his position as engineer in the same month. In 1844, when the question of wheel tread was causing ill-feeling, his premises were again damaged.

On 8 April 1847, after an illness, Sheasby retired, but was appointed consulting engineer, and George Baker Keeling became clerk at £250 p.a. He was a worthy successor to Sheasby, later becoming the secretary, and in 1871 'secretary and general manager.'

When the s & w & sbr was formed in 1879, G. B. Keeling resigned, but was elected to the board, and was managing director until his death on 28 February 1894, aged 80, at Severn House, Lydney; the directors, recording their regret, said simply 'His urbanity and kindliness of manner endeared him to all'. His son, George William, probably exerted the greatest force of any single personality in the company's long history, as will be seen.

CHAPTER 3

The Main Line Tramroad

The main line as conceived extended from Lydney to the Wye, but the high land about Mierystock was akin to a frontier, for the section thence to the Wye was much less used than that to Lydney, and traffic between the rivers was light; the line north of Mierystock was in fact of branch status and will accordingly be described in Chapter 4.

At Mierystock, the line was to run in a deep cutting, but the sides kept slipping, and the committee decided in December 1810 to substitute a tunnel 'for opening the communication of the two lines'. Morgan contracted to complete this by 1 May 1811, at 4½ guineas per yd; it was to be 9 ft wide and 10 ft high 'from the bed of the rail'; the stone arch was to be loaded with spoil and have portals of dressed stone. In 1852 it was crossed by a disused bridge, so the back-filling was not carried up to the original level. The tunnel was about 200 yd long and ascended at 1 in 79 towards Lydbrook.

The Churchway branch curved to the main line in the Lydbrook direction at Mierystock, and Lydney traffic had to 'reverse' across the turnpike until 1847, when a new curve was put in, making the junction triangular. In 1865 the tunnel, in imminent danger of falling in, was opened out to a cutting 'to let the locomotive pass', a new line being laid at a higher level to improve access to the Churchway branch. This line improved the gradients from 1 in 20, 24 and 30* to a uniform 1 in 36, but the old line was retained. This tunnel should not be confused with the railway tunnel of 1874, a little to the north.

In 1856 the average gradient from Lydney to Parkend was 1 in 170, and from Parkend to Wimberry Jcn 1 in 110. Originating coal tonnages were: 190 tons at Cannop Bridge, 70 at Bicslade, 280 at

---

* Doubtless these refer to the 1847 curve.

Parkend, 30 at Whitecroft, and 80 from a point near Norchard. At Lydney harbour 700 tons was shipped daily, so apparently 50 tons came from beyond Wimberry.[1]

CARRYING THE TRAFFIC

The tramroads were no different in commercial principle from the turnpike roads—the company maintained the track, collected

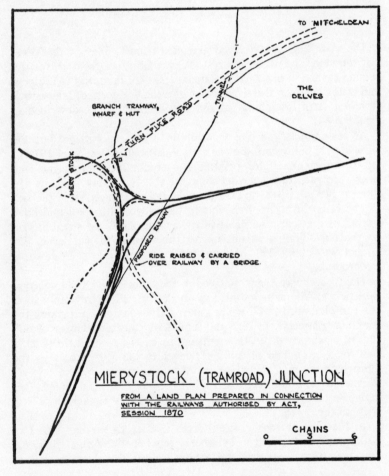

The final arrangement of Mierystock Jcn in tramroad days. The small triangle was formed by the addition of the south curve in 1847, and the longer south curve was laid in 1865

the tolls, and there, provided the users observed the simple rules, its interest ended; the loading and movement of traffic, provision of wagons and horses, and other practical details were the concern of the traders and hauliers.

The Act of 1809 laid down that mileposts or stones were to be erected 'and for ever maintained' to aid in the calculation of tolls and the line was to be open to all persons with proper wagons who were prepared to pay these. Fines were fixed for having loads projecting over the wagon sides so as to obstruct others passing, for obstructing the line with a wagon and for intent to avoid payment. Maximum tolls were fixed as follows:

Stone for public road repairs, manure ...	2d per ton per mile
Coal, coke, ore, building materials to Lydbrook or to Lower Forge, or intermediately	3s per ton for the whole distance
Coal, etc. to Howlers Slade or other branch for transport by road or railway towards Coleford or Monmouth	6d per ton for the whole distance
For the above materials to any place within the Forest except for Coleford or Monmouth as above	1s 6d per ton for the whole distance
All other goods	6d per ton per mile

The Act empowered the company to make bye-laws and levy fines. The first bye-laws were approved in October 1811, and additions were made subsequently.

Double track was provided between Parkend and Lydney from the beginning and all wagons going down to Lydney were to keep to the eastern side of the double track to the Dam Pool, and then to cross to the west side. In 1843, all wagons going down were to keep to the east side throughout, while from 1 May 1846 they were to use the west line. On single 'roads' (a term used commonly from the beginning instead of 'track' or 'line') all returning wagons were to give way to loaded wagons *en route* to the rivers 'and haul back to the nearest turnout'. Wagons remaining all night upon the line were to be left on 'the proper turnouts made for that purpose' and were to proceed when the gates were opened, or be 'turned over or removed from the road'. The gates were opened and closed as follows:

1 April to 30 September	...	5 a.m.	8 p.m.
1 October to 31 March	...	6 a.m.	7 p.m.

'Dangerous driving' was not unknown, and it was soon necessary to forbid any haulier 'trotting his horse upon the railway with any tram . . . or taking any tram down any of the branches faster than a horse can walk', or drawing wagons along, off the plates, while in 1830 the load for one team of horses had to be limited to nine wagons. The hauliers sometimes put too much faith in their lead animal, walking ahead or lagging behind their trams, and under a bye-law of 1840 all wagons were to have hauliers in attendance.

The weighing machines were situated at Lydney and Lydbrook. All loaded trams were weighed, a ticket was issued, the traders filled up a declaration detailing the consignments, and the ever-vigilant Sheasby was not slow to descend upon transgressors. He reported in 1833 that traders generally were carrying 2½ cwt more in each tram than was allowed, and in 1837 the wagons were still overloaded, especially with iron ore, leading to breakage of plates. As it was little use to make this discovery at the end of the journey, in 1838 a weighing machine and keeper's house were erected at Parkend. There were soon complaints that the machines erred on the company's side, and in 1811 the Lydney machine was adjusted to weigh 120 pounds to the cwt.

THE TOLLS AND THE TRAFFIC

The tolls were first fixed on 22 June 1809, and the proprietors, not to be caught unprepared, included rates for cider and beer, flour and grain. In January 1810 'back carriage' or return traffic of iron ore, manure, groceries, manufactured goods and liquors was en-visaged. The principal tolls fixed in July 1814 were well below the parliamentary maximum, i.e., for Low Delph coal 1s 6d per ton the entire distance, and High Delph coal 9d per ton. Specific tolls were reduced from time to time by granting 'drawbacks' (rebates) to encourage a new traffic, to meet competition, or occasionally to save a traffic from extinction. The company was permitted to re-cover unpaid tolls by confiscating wagons and selling the contents, and in 1813 Sheasby was directed thus to collect bad debts.

At the request of the Rev Henry Poole, the company carried free of charge the stone for St Paul's Church, near Parkend, providing a siding for the traffic in 1820. In 1833 cinders brought by the inhabit-ants of Whitecroft from Parkend for repairing the Bream—Yorkley road were carried at 3d per tram load of 35 cwt after the Crown surveyor had asked if they could be carried free, the committee insisting that turnouts be made to prevent interference with traffic.

THE SEVERN & WYE SCENE

(7) *Severn Bridge and station, from a watercolour by W. Key*
(8) *Lydbrook viaduct, about 1880, from a coloured* S & W & SBR *poster*

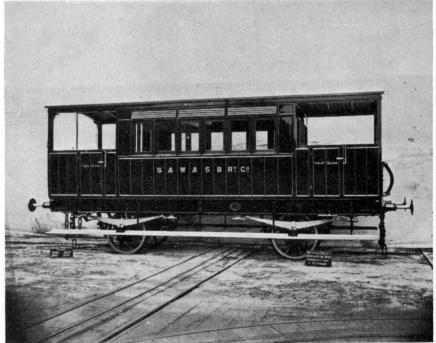

EARLY RAILWAY DAYS

(9) *Lydbrook viaduct in 1874. Contractors still at work, the station incomplete*

(10) *First-class saloon carriage No. 12, as repaired in 1889*

The collection of tolls as the wagons passed, only waived when a trader could provide a security or guarantee for credit, became difficult with increased traffic, and from 1 January 1839 monthly accounts were adopted. The sums outstanding in March indicate the large trade passing—they range from £42 (Soudley Iron Co.) to £750 (Park End Co.). In 1852 a toll of 1s 6d per ton was fixed for Thomas Watkins to carry Navy timber from Russell's Enclosure to the basin. It seems that little Navy timber was carried; in fact it was stated in the promotion of one of the Central line schemes that it was customarily taken down to Purton Pill.

In January 1822 several hauliers complained of their inability to pay fines and the committee, perhaps in New-Year mood, halved them. Two years later Samuel Gething bemoaned the hardship of a 20s fine for failure to declare a load of iron, and it was remitted, it being his first offence. William Ambrose was not so fortunate when, in 1826, the horrified Sheasby learned of his 'dragging with about a dozen horses without any carriage a very large timber tree along the road on Howler Slade for about 400 yd, which must have much injured the position of the rails and blocks'.

The tramroads passed through few centres of population, and no serious consideration of passenger traffic arose; the Act, unlike that of the Monmouth Railway, made no mention of such traffic. The miners and teamsters took advantage of passing wagons, and a bye-law of 1817 forbade riding upon a wagon, except those returning unloaded. The 'Pleasure Trams' (see Chapter 4) undoubtedly carried passengers, and there was some unofficial pleasure riding at week-ends, as a bye-law of 1823 prohibited using, or riding in, wagons on Sunday; an old photograph appears to show a jaunt of this nature.[2] The committee often concluded meetings by a journey in 'the Company's carriage' where circumstances called for an inspection, and this vehicle conveyed the directors behind the first tramroad locomotive on 16 November 1864.

In 1835 a Mr Hutchins of Whitecroft was granted permission to use a carriage prepared for the purpose upon the tramroad, to convey his family from their house to the nearest turnpike road, at a rate of 1s a week, but in 1837 his 'application to travel on the railway in a carriage' was refused. Riding or leading animals along the tramroad was a privilege confined to the proprietors, the Surveyor General, and local magistrates, but others covertly used those convenient ways. The clerk rode many miles for the company, and in 1848 he was given the horse, with £50 p.a. maintenance allowance.

C

It was vital to keep traffic moving; in 1847 the committee reminded G. B. Keeling to see that the snow ploughs and ice boat were ready for use during the winter, and in 1854 the *Gloucester Journal* commended the company for keeping the line open during a heavy snowfall. On 22 September 1869 a team belonging to the Forest of Dean Chemical Co. was drawing empty wagons down the tramroad between Parkend and Cannop when the lead horse, having no haulier in attendance, crossed over on to the broad-gauge railway, and was killed by a train on its way up the valley. A similar accident occurred in 1870, and a fence was erected between the tramroad and the railway.

THE 'ROAD'

The original gauge was 3 ft 6 in., and as recorded in Volume 2, this was quite probably that of the already partly built Bullo Pill line, and certainly that adopted a little later for the Monmouth Tramroad. Outram had recommended flanged-plate permanent way (devised by John Curr about 1776) consisting of cast-iron L-section rails 3 ft long, weighing about 37 lb. each. Outram died in 1805, and two years later Rennie, who had completed a plateway at Caldon Low in 1803, recommended plates weighing 42 lb. per yard in the Forest.

The Act stated that proper places were to be set out for wagons to 'turn, lie, or pass each other' and at road crossings the flange was not to exceed one inch in height above road level. The plates rested on stone blocks, each with one central hole, into which was driven an oak plug (probably octagonal, to prevent bursting of the block when the plug became wet). The plates had a countersunk notch in each end, forming a square hole when placed together, and an iron spike was driven through this hole into the plug, hence the term 'nail plate' later used by Keeling. Spikes can still be seen in surviving blocks at Darkhill and on the Oakwood Tramroad.

The contractors supplied all material except the plates, and had to guarantee their work for a year. The blocks were to weigh at least 160 lb., be at least 14 in. square by 7 in. thick, with a hole 5 in. deep and 1¼ in. diameter. The nails were to be 5 in. long, three to the pound, and the 'road' was to be backed level with the plates 2 ft wide each side and filled between the 'flanches' with small stone, gravel or furnace cinders.

Hill & Hopkins, Blaenavon ironworks, offered 'flanch rails' 3 ft long, 42 lb. weight, of good grey cast-iron and guaranteed for 12

months in July 1809, and 1,000 tons, delivered at Newport at £7 5s
per ton, at nine months' credit, were ordered in April 1810. They
came down by tramroad and canal to Newport, whence 'Owner
Browne' offered to bring them to Brockweir at 5s per ton. Brockweir
was the highest point on the Wye for vessels of 80 to 90 tons,
cargoes being transhipped there into barges suitable for the shallow water. In November 1810 Parry was asked to forward a new
set of rail turnout patterns to Blaenavon, 'to get 12 setts . . . cast
immediately and forward to Lydney by the first vessel'. A more
robust plate was supplied for special use, as in April 1811 the
s & w had about 50 tons of 'heavy rails' surplus and asked Hill &
Hopkins to take them back or exchange them.

Throughout its tramroad era the company supplied plates for
branches to traders—at first gratuitously, but by October 1811 it
was decided that as the practice was often abused, none should be
delivered save on payment and to communicate with the s & w.
Blaenavon supplied the plates for some years, but in 1821 the
Pidcocks (Lydney Forges) and the Tredegar Iron Co. secured part of
the trade. In 1822 Sheasby reported that the Blaenavon iron was too
soft; in 1823 it was resolved to purchase in future rails made of
'foundry iron', and Samuel Hewlett of Ayleford Foundry offered
these at £7 per ton, delivered where needed, taking the old plates at
£4 per ton—in earlier years broken plates were often repaired.
Hewlett supplied almost all the rails for ten years, but in 1833 the
Yniscedwyn Iron Co., Swansea, secured the contract and had some
difficulty in keeping up an adequate supply: 'there not being one
plate in stock at the wharf since last week' emphasises their fragility.
In 1839 its offer was accepted for plates 'from the Anthracite Coal';
it was proposed to lay five tons from Yniscedwyn and five tons
from Hewlett for experiments on comparative wear, and the Welsh
contract was renewed in 1842.

New designs for plates and chairs were studied in 1845, the first
mention of chairs on the s & w, and in 1848 the 'change of line for
heavy traffic' was approved, wrought-iron plates being introduced.
They were used in all renewals after 1853, first in 6-ft lengths, later
9 ft. The chairs were cast with a dovetail seat for the tramplate, one
side having a curved hollow inner face for a wooden wedge or key.
Two tapered bosses were cast at 8½ in. centres, and 'dogged' into
holes in the blocks, probably with lead.

On 21 April 1853 G. B. Keeling reported that wrought-iron plates
were laid on 993 yd of line and 563 yd had been relaid with old
castings. Between Lydney basin and Mierystock there remained

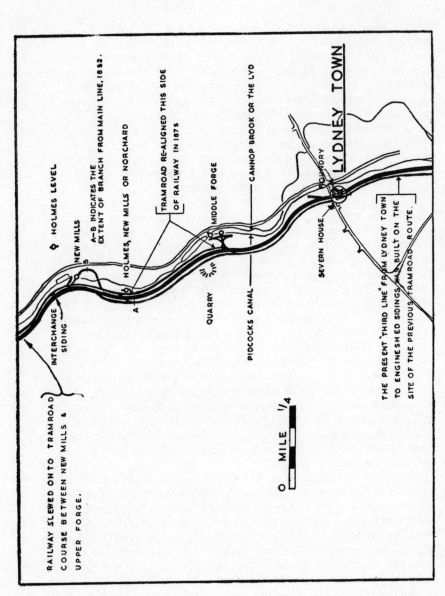

RAILWAY SLEWED ONTO TRAMROAD
COURSE BETWEEN NEW MILLS &
UPPER FORGE.

INTERCHANGE
SIDING

HOLMES LEVEL

NEW MILLS

A—B INDICATES THE
EXTENT OF BRANCH FROM MAIN LINE, 1852.

TRAMROAD REALIGNED THIS SIDE
OF RAILWAY IN 1875

HOLMES, NEW MILLS OR NORCHARD

B

A

MIDDLE FORGE

CANNOP BROOK OR THE LYD

QUARRY

PIDCOCKS CANAL

SEVERN HOUSE

FOUNDRY

LYDNEY TOWN

THE PRESENT "THIRD LINE" FROM LYDNEY TOWN
TO ENGINESHED SIDINGS, WAS BUILT ON THE
SITE OF THE PREVIOUS TRAMROAD ROUTE.

O   MILE   ¼

Map No. 1. Lydney Town

four miles of nail-plates, worn and out of gauge, and needing replacement with wrought-iron, especially as heavier wagons were contemplated; 2¾ miles of main line were laid with cast-iron plates in chairs, in fair condition. Keeling soon replaced 1,653 yd of nail-plates with wrought-iron, but the remainder continued to be troublesome because of rains and increased traffic.

By April 1864 the whole main line was laid with wrought-iron plates weighing 40 lb. per yard, in 14-lb. cast-iron chairs, on stone blocks at a longitudinal pitch of 2 ft 6 in. to 3 ft 0 in., the shorter pitch being a fairly late development.

The locomotives introduced in 1864 really required edge rails, for the plates tended to clog with stones, but to expect all the traders to equip their wagons with flanged wheels, whilst maintaining trade, was impractical. This difficulty had been overcome by the Monmouthshire Railway & Canal Co. with a combined rail and tram plate, and on 21 March 1866 G. W. Keeling reported on gradual conversion to an edge railway using such rails. It was agreed to order 25 tons, and quotations were still being considered in January 1868, but as the purchases were very small, and there is no record of the locomotives having flanged wheels fitted, it is probable that this stop-gap scheme was overtaken by the railways; these combined plates may well have been used on a line from Lydney Jcn to the harbour (see Chapter 12).

In 1894 the GWR became responsible (*via* the Joint Committee) for the maintenance of the surviving tramroads and introduced a heavier chair. The Bicslade track in 1951 consisted in general of angle irons 4½ in. x 2¼ in., ½ in. thick and 4 yd long; where it crossed the road, a channel section was used, forming a trough. On the Churchway branch the blocks were at about 2 ft 6 in. pitch, with three holes, one the original central plug hole, the others for the chairs. In later years wooden sleepers were used to some extent.

THE WAGONS

Outram recommended wagons carrying from 30 to 40 cwt each, a horse taking six or eight, containing 10 or 12 tons of coals, from Serridge summit to the head of Lydbrook incline and returning with an equal number of empty wagons, in two hours. By the 1809 Act, wagons were to be constructed to company regulations, to be advertised on toll houses. The toll collectors were empowered to gauge, weigh or measure wagons quarterly, and each was to bear the owner's name, address, and wagon number in white paint.

Under bye-laws of 1811, wagons were to have four wheels not less than 1 ft 9 in. diameter, and not more than 3 ft 6 in. in gauge between the wheels. Maximum loads were fixed at 20 cwt for normal wagons, 35 cwt (2 tons if the load was in one piece) for a wagon with axles 1 yd apart, and two or more had to be used for one load of over two tons. These maxima were modified to 30 cwt, 47 cwt, and 50 cwt in 1832, but the tare of the wagon was included. In 1835 the axle centres were fixed at 3 ft minimum.

In December 1840 the gauge was altered to 3 ft 7 in., and in October 1843 to 3 ft 8 in. This inch-by-inch widening suggests bowing to a gradual spreading of the blocks rather than inspired policy. G. W. Keeling's drawing of a wagon, dated March 1856, scales 3 ft 8¼ in. between the inner faces of the wheels, and the section through the track gives a dimension of 3 ft 8 in., apparently intended to be between the outer faces of the vertical flanges.[3]

Overloaded wagons, with narrow wheel rims, caused grooving of the plates, and a bye-law forbade the use of wheels less than ⅞ in. wide at the rim, after 1 October 1840. Edward Protheroe protested, the traders made little or no effort to re-wheel their wagons, and in due course an offender was summoned. The magistrates at Lydney held the bye-laws to be insufficient for a conviction, and in 1841 they were re-worded, stipulating that all wagons should have four wheels, minimum diameter 1 ft 9 in., minimum bearing width ⅞ in., maximum gauge 3 ft 7 in., and minimum wheelbase 3 ft 0 in. In May the traders stated that a ⅝ in. rim was quite adequate, but they were refused another year's grace. As a last straw, Trotter Thomas & Co. had begun using two new wagons with only ⅜ in. rims and Sheasby was told to enforce fines already incurred by them (for Richard James, the haulier) and Protheroe, and to take further proceedings.

In October 1843 some traders (particularly Trotter Thomas) were using wheels 'in opposition to the gauge authorised'; it was amended to 3 ft 8 in., but in 1844 the Park End Coal Co. was still using wheels 'under the lawful gauge'.

The company assisted the traders in 1842 by purchasing new wagons for hire, but they were sold in 1844. After 1852, the purchase and hire of wagons again became common practice. In 1853 G. B. Keeling proposed a larger heavier wagon. A new 'tram carriage' had been completed, ten more ordered from Parkes & Baker at £17 each, and let at £4 p.a. each. By October, 20 improved wagons had been ordered for coal, and 20 others, costing £10 each, chiefly for iron ore, some 'already in use and highly approved'—

but they earned only £2 10s p.a. each, the company keeping them in repair.

The stock of company tram wagons rose to about 270 in 1871, falling thereafter. It is hardly possible to estimate the number of private wagons, but there must have been many hundreds, one large 'park' surviving at New Fancy in 1947. An iron wagon carrying a screw-press, for bending the later steel rails, on Bicslade wharf in 1961, was probably a GWR refinement.

The larger blocks of stone had to be carried on two wagons. Some traders provided two four-wheeled frames coupled by a bar-link and pins, carrying a timber platform with a pivot pin to each bogie, and it was said of two Trotter Thomas wagons in 1841, 'each of the eight wheels of such waggons had but ⅜ in. instead of ⅞ in. bearing upon the plates'. Not true bogie wagons, they were probably as near as any tramroad ever got to such luxuries. Wagons trading *via* Churchway had axles with adjustable cotters, which with the insertion of washers, permitted through running over the Bullo Pill line,[4] the gauge of which, in later years, was roughly 4 ft 0 in.

Outram had suggested the use of iron slippers or sledges, chained to the wagon-sides, and put under the wheels when needed, for braking the wagons.[5] In 1823 it was forbidden to 'sprag' any wheel other than by using shoes, but more recently the general method adopted was thrusting a billet of wood through the spokes, or on stone wagons, sledging so that the rear wheels were clear of the plates. A bye-law of 1813 required shafts to be used in hauling loaded wagons on steep sections.

Coal wagons opened at one end when tipped at Lydney harbour. The drawing of 1856 showed a typical wagon with 2 ft 3 in.-diameter wheels, while cast-iron wheels examined at Point Quarry had diameters of about 2 ft 0 in. and 1 ft 9 in. with eight and ten spokes respectively, the wheelbase being about 3 ft 3 in. and the rail gauge about 3 ft 10 in. The animals used included horses, ponies and even mules.

THE MAIN LINE TODAY

The railway followed the tramroad closely between Lydney and Wimberry Jcn, but as both were operated simultaneously for some years, the tramroad land was retained. From Lydney Harbour the route was largely occupied by sidings to Lydney Town, where the tramroad passed behind the goods yard. The original formation continues on the down (i.e. the west) side; near New Mills it crosses

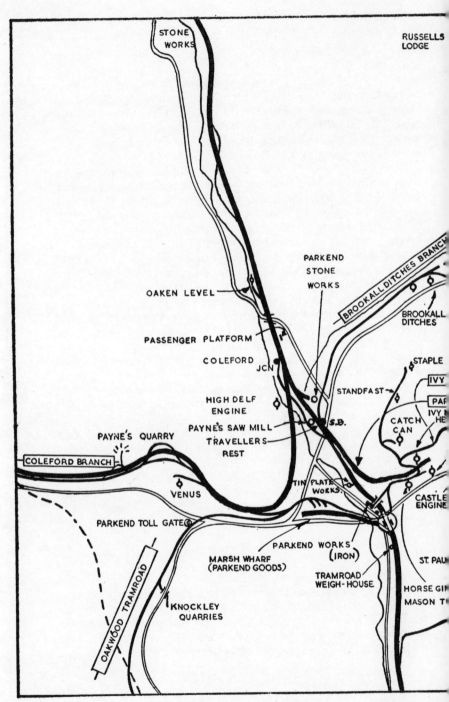

STONE WORKS

RUSSELLS LODGE

PARKEND STONE WORKS

OAKEN LEVEL

BROOKALL DITCHES BRANCH

BROOKALL DITCHES

PASSENGER PLATFORM

COLEFORD JCN

STANDFAST

STAPLE

IVY

PAR

IVY N HE

HIGH DELF ENGINE

S.D.

CATCH CAN

PAYNE'S QUARRY

PAYNE'S SAW MILL

TRAVELLERS REST

COLEFORD BRANCH

VENUS

TIN PLATE WORKS

CASTLE ENGINE

PARKEND TOLL GATE

PARKEND WORKS (IRON)

ST. PAU

MARSH WHARF (PARKEND GOODS)

TRAMROAD WEIGH-HOUSE

HORSE GIN MASON T

OAKWOOD TRAMROAD

KNOCKLEY QUARRIES

Map No. 2. P

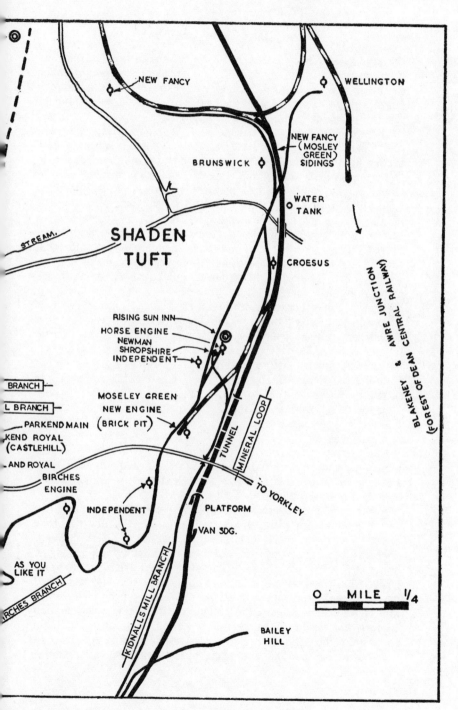

Moseley Green

the railway and is partly covered by Norchard colliery, but beyond it curves to the site of an exchange siding. The tramroad continued on the up side, the railway being slewed on to its course to improve curvature. At Upper Forge the shells of three small buildings survive, occupied by undergrowth and trees.

There was a forge at 'Lidenie' in 1221. Three forges, Upper, Middle and Lower, were leased in 1814 by John James of Redbrook. In 1814 Sheasby was instructed to make connections to Upper and Middle Forges, and a short branch was made in 1818 to Lower Forge, connecting to a private line. James probably erected New Mills in 1824. By 1858 T. & W. Allaway were operating the plants, producing tin-plates, and Richard Thomas took over in March 1875. In 1887 the yearly traffic between Upper and Lower Forges was about 4,200 tons in process of manufacture, and 5,200 tons of coal to or from New Mills. Upper Forge was dismantled by 1891, soon followed by Middle Forge, but Lower Forge continued to operate until November 1957.

Beyond Upper Forge the tramroad crossed the railway twice as it approached Tufts Jcn, but by the Act of 1853 it was re-aligned on the present railway course on this section. Northward the course, on the down side, has been obscured by a former siding and by Whitecroft down platform; a branch to a brickyard near Phipps Bottom was shown on plans of 1852, possibly the same as one shown by Bryant in 1823 to Grove colliery.

Beyond Parkend station, the tramroad ran alongside the single-line railway through the restricted 'covered way', and up to Wimberry it was on the down side. John Protheroe was developing Whitelea colliery in 1815. A branch to the pit was gated near the main line, and marked 'old tramway' in 1852, while in 1861 Nash and Henderson borrowed s & w plates to make a new branch, which had been removed by 1878.

Railway sidings covered the course between Speech House Road and Wimberry Jcn (near which, as late as 1869, a new tramroad branch was made, to H. R. Lückes's Rose-in-Hand colliery), but it appears again beyond a fence, and passes Old Bob's pumping engine house; it passed under the railway embankment twice by temporary bridges, built to maintain tramroad communication and later filled up. The course turns sharply across the Cannop Brook, the tip of this curve being beneath the embankment. The first Speculation colliery was inside this curve, and a 'cut-off' was laid to maintain communication. The tramroad curves north, passing the shaft of the second Speculation, and stone blocks, hitherto rare, become numerous. Beyond, a stone bank was built in recent years to load coal from the third Speculation into lorries, but water difficulties caused abandonment in 1956.

The site of Mierystock tramroad junction was obliterated by colliery sidings, but just past the footbridge over the railway cutting the course can be picked up approaching the main road. The route northwards is described in Chapter 4.

The Branch Tramroads

IN THE DEPTHS OF THE FOREST

There were 12 branch tramroads, mostly tapping minerals from the recesses of the Forest, including the Mierystock—Lydbrook—Bishopswood section and the privately-owned Oakwood and Dyke's branches. In addition, scores of sidings and short branches served particular mines, quarries and works. The branches varied considerably in character, purpose and longevity, but all had features of interest, and most have left behind more enduring traces than the main line, being rarely disturbed by the later railways.

Except in the case of Churchway (and probably Moseley Green), the tram locomotives passed the branches by, for they were mostly tortuous and steep. Various proposals for converting branches to railways met with no success, and they were gradually superseded by adjacent railway routes, or abandoned; three, however (Howlers Slade, Wimberry Slade and Bicslade), remained in use until comparatively recent years, down to wharves on the main line.

Proceeding from Lydney into the Forest, the first off-shoot was DYKE'S branch (about ¾-mile), laid as late as 1857, from Tufts to Princess Royal colliery, Thomas Dyke preparing the earthworks and the s & w laying the track. Dyke's traffic probably began in November, when a wharf at the harbour was let to him, and Park Hill coal level was also served (its arch is dated 10 December 1857). A potential route to the Oakwood valley, the branch was conveyed to the s & w on 8 August 1870, and later converted.

The KIDNALL'S MILL (or MOSELEY GREEN) branch, some 2¾ miles long, had no construction time limit, and many years elapsed before it was laid, as the central district was little developed. Mineral owners there continually complained of lack of facilities, and when Protheroe demanded action the company could no longer procrastinate. Sheasby was told in April 1841 to start at Phelps Meadow and build south, but heavy construction, costing £3,570, delayed completion until September 1844.

In 1843 the S & W had obtained a licence to extend the branch 2¼ miles to Foxes Bridge, effective for 26 years, at an annual rent of £35, the tramroad to be levelled and restored within six months if traffic ceased. Some work was done in 1845-46, but no real effort was made to complete the extension, Foxes Bridge colliery being unopened. Brunswick and Wellington collieries were not particularly successful, being closed in 1850 and 1852 respectively, due, it was said in 1865, to the high S & W tolls. A new line with easier curves, from Tufts to Pillowell Level, authorised in 1853, was completed in October 1856. The superseded route from Whitecroft was repaired in 1866, as it was more direct for the Patent Fuel Company there.

A branch to New Fancy colliery was made in 1859 by the Park End Coal Co., which in 1867 obtained a licence for a broad-gauge branch to the FOD Central Railway, crossing the unbuilt S & W Foxes Bridge extension, for which incursion it offered a rent of 10s p.a.—scant compensation for the considerable tonnage (about 80,000 yearly), in danger of being lost to the abhorred Central line. S & W protests were unavailing, but in 1869 the tramroad still had a large part of the traffic.

The Kidnall's branch was superseded by the Mineral Loop line, and the Commissioners sanctioned abandonment in December 1874. Much later a horse tramway was laid, partly on the tramroad, by Phipps Brothers, from New Whitecroft colliery to a coal wharf, and this survived in 1920.

The original junction is covered by Whitecroft up platform and a pin factory. The route proceeds due east, climbing on an embankment, with Pillowell viaduct, which the 1856 deviation crossed, on the right. The tramroad turns sharply north, beside the railway route, and crosses a road. A short cutting (originally a tramroad tunnel, opened out in 1862) is spanned by a footbridge, and the tramroad diverges to the left of the railway, with woods on either side, climbing steadily but easily. The line passes under the Yorkley road by a short tunnel a few yards west of the railway tunnel, the keystone on the north side being marked '1842'. Beyond, the route has been covered by a colliery tip, a railway siding and then the roadway, to the junction with the Birches branch, beyond which it forks, one line going to New Fancy while the other, obliterated by the railway embankment, terminates at Wellington colliery, now a mound in the scrub land of Brandrick's Green.

The BIRCHES branch left the main line south of Parkend, and passed through Oakenhill Inclosure to Birches Well, Independent, and other coal pits. The company tried to relinquish its powers for separate branches to the Birches and to Moseley Green, and to make one line, *via* the Birches. Sheasby sent a plan to Lord Glenbirvie's office in March 1812, requesting an early answer as the Parliamentary time limit was pressing and, to his agreeable surprise, the plan was approved on 25 April.

By 1820 it was necessary to lengthen the turnouts to accommodate 20 wagons, in 1827 Protheroe was developing Birches Well, and in 1835 the branch terminated at Newmans Shropshire coalpit, near the Shaden Tuft. Atkinson showed the Kidnall's Mill branch on his map of 1842, joining the Birches branch. The Birches pit was not in use but its atmospheric engine was used to pump water from Independence South, worked by Protheroe. Some 28 tons were raised daily from the 105-yd shaft and sent to Lydney.

In 1844 the company agreed that the Park End Coal Co. could use the tramplates lying on the branch 'leading from the Horse Engine to the new branch now laid up from Kidnell's Mill to near Phelps Meadow', and the branch was disused by about 1849; it was shown on plans of 1852, but only as far as the Birches. The Commissioners approved abandonment in 1874, and the track had been removed by 1877.

The tramroad climbs sharply out of the railway cutting—the fence makes a turn in its memory—and curves away into a cutting; the numerous blocks have a single hole, showing that the track was never relaid with chairs, and the marks where the plates wore into the stone are clear. The route passes through conifer plantations, profoundly isolated, bearing N.E. to run parallel to the Parkend —Yorkley road. At the end of a broad avenue through the trees, the route performs a series of loops, trees having been planted right across the formation. It can be followed, with difficulty, in the thick brown gloom, to a cutting, crossed by a path, giving the impression of a more than desolate dead-end terminus. The course continues as a broad path to the Yorkley road, crossed on the level; beyond, it passes the ruins of Moseley Green New Engine colliery. The rotting sleepers of the railway branch are now underfoot, and ahead lies the open expanse of Moseley Green. The railway bore away to the right, but the tramroad continues straight, marked by blocks in front of the 'Rising Sun'—no picture-postcard inn this, but a weather-beaten, isolated little miners' saloon with the dark woods of the Shaden Tuft a stone's throw away. The route continues in a shallow wooded cutting, past a lonely chapel, and crosses the Blakeney road to join the Moseley Green tramroad.

PARKEND—A TRAMROAD CENTRE

Parkend, now a forest-girt hamlet nestling in a natural basin, was once an industrial centre and a focal point of the s & w system, four branches converging from Ivy Moor Head, Brookhall Ditches, Milkwall and Oakwood to feed traffic into the ironworks and on to the double tracks down to Lydney.

The ancient ironworks at Parkend were suppressed by the Crown about 1674. In 1799 a furnace was built on a new site, but soon fell idle, and in April 1824 Edward Protheroe was contemplating re-opening it after Teague's successful experiment in smelting with coke. However, Protheroe leased the works, with iron mines, to the new Forest of Dean Iron Company; by October the erection of a new furnace had been commenced, and it was necessary for the s & w to lay in a branch, production beginning in 1826.

A feature of Parkend was a short artificial tunnel, the 'covered way', created because the s & w tramroad was in a cutting and the furnaces were fed from lines which passed over it. In 1866 production was upwards of 300 tons of pig-iron per week, using 600 tons of ore from the Oakwood and China Engine mines, and the Perseverance and Findall mines to the east.

In 1875 the Iron Co. sold out to Edwin Crawshay and he also acquired the tin-plate works (erected in 1851 and operated by T. & W. Allaway) which he soon closed, and later dismantled. There was little work on hand and on 4 August 1877 the last furnace was blown out. The depression had been accentuated by a fault in the China Mine, the trams being often filled with rubbish and ore spread on top to simulate a full load. Crawshay had purchased Robin Hood mine, between Coleford and Staunton, but the Coleford Railway was uncompleted, and cart haulage had increased production costs.[1] The 'covered way' was removed in 1898, the furnaces having been demolished in 1890.

About 1812 Edward Protheroe, with Thomas Waters, purchased the majority of his uncle John Protheroe's collieries for 20,000 guineas, and soon obtained numerous licences for developing them.[2] In 1841 the Parkend pits were producing some 300 tons daily. an atmospheric pumping engine labouring mightily at 14 strokes a minute.[3] By 1848 the Parkend and New Fancy collieries were leased to T. Nicholson and sent out 72,000 tons annually, supplying over 1,000 tons per month to the FOD Iron Co.[4]

THE PARKEND BRANCHES

The MILKWALL (or DARKHILL) branch brought iron ore from the Milkwall area to Parkend, served collieries and wandered through large quarries. It was under construction early in 1812 and followed a hard, tortuous, hillside route. The proximity of the quarries at Futterhill led to many disputes with the Yarworth family in early years, their quarrying frequently 'destroying' the tramroad. In 1814 a Mr Glover took rails without leave and extended the branch from Dark Hill down to Blanches Level, whereupon the company blandly ordered that 'same will remain as the Company's property and free for the use of the public'.

In April 1814 a Mr Phillips requested that the branch to Darkhill be extended to meet a 'junction branch now formed from the angle above the Futtral Quarry to the Monmouth Railway', to be open to the public on payment of tolls, and Sheasby was instructed to proceed without delay. It is said that no physical junction was made between the two lines, but that an interchange wharf was made by the roadside, near Winnells Deep Level.[5] This connection was soon allowed to fall derelict.

In 1819 Sheasby was directed to extend the original branch about 300 yd to serve David Mushet's new Darkhill Furnace, and in 1824 he was instructed to renew the branch to the place to which it had once been formed 'but had since been allowed to get out of order', as Protheroe was sinking iron mines near Milkwall.

Robert Forester Mushet set up the Forest Steelworks about 1848 near Milkwall for special steel production; here, in 1856, he made Bessemer's process for cheap steel practical by adding spiegeleisen to the poor-quality product of the converter.[6] Bulk production ceased in 1871.

In 1860 some of the worst curves were being smoothed out, and in 1864 three iron mines, Old Sling, Easter and Dean's Meend, produced together over 40,000 tons. In 1872 E. R. Payne's quarries were producing a large tonnage for Birkenhead, Cardiff and Newport Docks, which was hauled nearly a mile by road from Darkhill, then on the tramroad to Parkend, where 3d per ton was charged to load it by crane on the broad gauge to Lydney. The cost was 4s 1d per ton for the seven miles, yet Yorkshire stone was sold in Gloucester at 3s 4d per foot cheaper than Dean stone. Osman Barratt's iron ore from the Easter pit, however, 'kept to the tramway altogether' down to Lydney.[7]

GOODS TRAINS

(11) *West-bound train at Drybrook Road, 1922*

(12) *No. 2044 begins the long climb from Coleford Jcn with the early-morning branch goods, 1948*

(13) *North-bound p.w. train at Parkend, with 'Dean' 0—6—0 No. 2515, 1947*

PASSENGER TRAINS

(14) *Up train at Parkend, 1922*

(15) *Dean 0—6—0 No. 2322 on a diverted Bristol—Cardiff train passing Sharpness, 1950*

The tramroad was in operation until the railway was completed, as witness a short curved brick tunnel under the railway at Point Quarry, and reference to a temporary wooden bridge at Milkwall. The Commissioners sanctioned abandonment on 16 March 1876, probably upon conversion (delayed due to lack of money) of the Sling branch, which had earlier been diverted slightly at Milkwall to terminate at a tip over a siding. A short stretch was left at Point Quarry, and as late as 1890 this was extended to the railway bridge across the Coleford road, whence David & Co. continued it into their quarries.

At Parkend, the branch followed the course of the later Goods branch, then crossed the road to run in front of the present-day sawmill (where blocks remain in plenty), before climbing away from the Coleford road, to a course alongside the railway, a siding serving Venus colliery. The railway was on a sharp curve, on an embankment spanning the mouth of a pleasant little hollow in the hillside, sheltering several houses, and the original tramroad passed round the back of them; later it was re-aligned to avoid the loop, and when the railway was built the tramroad was diverted again, south of the railway.[8] Further on, a similar diversion was made. A steep incline down to the road served a pit, and the main tramroad passed under the railway into Point Quarry. The later route is clear, alongside and north of the railway to David's Quarry, but the original course, south of the railway, is largely lost under Futterhill siding, although it can be picked up again where it crosses the railway just before the Coleford road bridge. The course curves sharply to cross the road, then climbs back towards the railway, with traces of a steep siding down to the ruins of the Darkhill ironworks. At the approach to the Forest works the formation has been destroyed by quarrying, but beyond it turns sharply across the railway, the abutments of the bridge remaining, then proceeds to Milkwall, where it curves sharply towards the ochre works and merges with the Sling branch.

David Mushet built up a little empire of coal and iron mines to serve his ironworks. In 1825 he secured a licence for the OAK-WOOD TRAMROAD, nearly 2½ miles long from a level named Oakwood or Oakwood Land and from quarries near Drybrook, to join the Milkwall branch near Parkend, the line to be completed before 25 March 1827, and open to the public on payment of tolls. The cost was about £1,500. James & Greenham (of Parkend ironworks) extended the tramroad to their China Engine and New China Level iron mines, running 'on the waste of the Forest', under

D

a licence of 1855, and in July the s & w special committee, visiting the Oakwood line, found it very much out of repair.

The Oakwood valley's rich iron ore was attracting attention from outside the Forest, and in July 1856 the Ebbw Vale Co. was about to put Bromley Hill furnace in blast, had opened a colliery at Drybrook, was opening an iron mine, and intended to erect another furnace when railway facilities were available.[9] In 1865 Oakwood Mill iron level produced nearly 6,500 tons, whilst New China produced only 410 tons.

In 1871 the s & w proposed to acquire the tramroad and convert it. It was surprised to hear that the FOD Iron Co. was satisfied with its line, and objected to the purchase, together with the Commissioners of Woods and the GWR. The s & w pointed out that it no longer served one gale* only, and its Act of 1872 authorised purchase by agreement, but plans for linking the Oakwood and Coleford railway branches were shelved, and the power was never exercised.

By 1872 Flourmill colliery was established beside the tramroad, also the Oakwood chemical works, while Bromley Hill furnace had been out of use for many years. Parkend ironworks were closed in 1877, ore subsequently being taken to the wharf at Parkend and loaded into railway trucks. China Engine and Princess Louise pits were closed in 1885, but in 1889 teams of horses were hauling heavy loads of ore from the pits nearer Parkend. The line beyond the foundry was removed by 1901, when only one of the four tips remained at Parkend wharf. Traffic continued until about 1907-1908, mainly ore to Parkend wharf and bar iron to Oakwood foundry, while Knockiey quarries were still worked. The track was removed before 1914 but the foundry, quarries and chemical works continued in use for a time, the chemical traffic being handled, surprisingly enough, by cart and pack-mule, a reversion to pre-tramroad days.

The route leaves the Milkwall tramroad just beyond Parkend sawmills and runs beside the road to Parkend toll-gate house, beyond which it crosses the Bream road to an independent course. On the left are the remains of three tunnels under the road, to Knockley quarries; the route enters a lengthy cutting, crossed by a stone arch which carried the Flourmill colliery tramway, beyond which are the buildings of the chemical works, partly in use as an electric sub-station.

The course, well marked by blocks, runs in the wooded valley of Oakwood Bottom. On the right, in the hillside, are the remains of Bromley Hill furnace, and the Milkwall road is crossed near the

* A grant of mining rights from the Crown.

pleasant Oakwood Inn. The route runs between low stone walls for a way, with plenty of spiked blocks, and the small, ruined foundry was on the right, dated '1852'. The valley narrows gradually and the course passes the remains of several workings to terminate at China Engine pit.

The IVY MOOR HEAD branch was built without delay, and without authority, for in October 1810 Parry was told to lay a turn-out on it, and one at Lydney Pill—obviously coal awaited shipment. In March 1811 the line needed repairing and in 1813 the s & w obtained a licence from the Crown to legalise the branch. Protheroe set about improving the Parkend pits with characteristic energy. Licences of 1827 permitted further pumping and winding engines at Ivy Moor Head, Parkend Main and Parkend Royal, and also a 1,500-yd branch from the s & w to the Royal pits.

The s & w relinquished the licence of 1813 in 1828, 'the said branch having become useless'; it had been taken up and re-aligned by the Park End Coal Co. in 1821 and was carrying coal to the ironworks, Protheroe using it as his 'private road' on the strength of his licence, without paying tolls. In 1829 he agreed to pay £20 p.a. for its use, and it became the s & w's 'public road'.

In 1835 the branch had tortuous sidings to Parkend Main, Royal, Catch Can, Standfast and Staple pits, and Parkend ironworks. A direct connection across the main line, taking ore from the Oakwood valley into the furnaces over the 'covered way', is shown on Roberts's map of c. 1840. In 1877 the line still pursued its winding way to the Royal pit (then Castlehill colliery), but it had been removed by 1901.

Estimates were sought in March 1811 for completing the BROOK-HALL DITCHES branch, about half-a-mile long. In 1824 the Park End Coal Co., due to stoppage of its Birches pit, was obliged to re-open its abandoned work at Brookhall Ditches. It requested Sheasby to replace the rails, but as its own manager had removed these because 'they would never want to use it again', the s & w decided that the coal company should pay for reinstatement, being reimbursed from its own tolls—a shrewd method used by the s & w in such cases to avoid fruitless expense.

The s & w obtained a licence in 1837 for an extension of about 2¼ miles to Foxes Bridge, and about £930 was spent on it until 1841, when the Kidnall's Mill branch was being made, offering a more direct outlet and avoiding the busy Parkend district. The s & w accordingly applied for a licence to extend the new line. By November 1842 the FODR had withdrawn objections to this substitution 'in lieu of the line at present formed . . . from Foxes Bridge to Brookhall Ditches', and a licence of 1843 authorised the extension of the Kidnall's branch to the north-east corner of the new Acorn Patch Inclosure and thence 'along the line already formed to Foxes Bridge', the 1837 licence being surrendered. Clearly much work had been done on the extension, but it is unlikely that track was ever laid, as no record exists of its use, and the Foxes Bridge pit in question was never opened.

In 1868 the Park End Coal Co. (which treated this line with scant respect) had erected a platform across it (probably Brookhall Ditches loading bank—see Chapter 7). The Commissioners authorised abandonment in 1874, and the plates had been removed by 1878.

There is no trace of the tramroad at the junction, as the stone mills covered it, and beyond is the New Road. A path between houses on the north side leads onto the course, which runs in woods north of the Moseley Green road. To the left is a large spoil mound and from it protrude two stone pit-shafts. The ground slopes away sharply to the left, to Brookways Ditch, and the route continues through forest on the hillside, to terminate near the road, by 'Woodside' house.

THREE LONG-LIVED TRAMROADS

The BICSLADE branch was completed within its time limit of June 1812, and by December 1814 had suffered from the Foresters' free and easy ways—one Moxham had opened a level, taken up some rails and crossed the 'road' without consent. In 1825 the FOD Iron Co. made a dam against the embankment on which the branch left the main line, creating the picturesque Cannop Ponds to work water wheels, and by 1841 the branch served three collieries in addition to the quarries, combined production being 70 tons daily.

An accident, rare on the tramroads, occurred in 1873, when a mare belonging to Payne, a quarry owner, was killed owing, he said, to the 'hollow state' of the line. The company, suspecting that the cause was rather overloaded trams overpowering the team, and quarry flood water washing the ballast away, paid £30 but cautioned Payne on both scores. The line was extended for short distances from time to time, as the quarries developed, at their owners' request, the S & W generally supplying the plates, and the owners doing the rest; on one such occasion, in 1855, the company insisted that the wagons should have at least 1¼ in.-wide wheel rims, due to the steep gradient and heavy loads. Several licences were granted in the 1890s to various owners, for extensions around the Bixhead quarries.

The tramroad gave way grudgingly to road transport. The last load of stone, weighing 8½ tons, was brought down the ¾-mile tramroad on 25 July 1944; in June 1946 the line was still in regular use for coal traffic from a pit near Bixhead, a report referring to it as 'Mr G. H. Jones's siding', but by November this traffic had ceased.

By 1947, motor lorries carrying stone along the upper section had damaged the track severely, only the blocks remaining in position. Track was preserved round Bixhead quarry, and two flat wagons were used to run stone to the nearby shaping shops, while at the other end a short stretch continued in use from the stone-works (established by Turner & Son in 1901) on to Bicslade siding wharf. The motive power here was a farm tractor or mechanical dumper, so that to a modest degree the tramroad had been modernised, but man-power was also used. From a point near Bicslade Land Level the lorries took a more convenient course for the works, and the track was in good order (the road crossing being laid with steel channel to form a trough) until about July 1952, when it was lifted. Substantial track remains, largely buried, survived on the wharf in 1961.

The HOWLERS SLADE branch ran parallel with the Speech House road, but impressively above it, for most of its 1-mile course. It was due for completion in June 1812, but it was not until December 1811 that Sheasby prepared estimates. In addition to various pits and quarries, the branch served two other industries. By 1835 a chemical works was established at Cannop Bridge, and in 1880 it was producing acids from oak loppings and from Mount Etna brimstone.[10] By 1901 the siding was removed and the works, latterly engaged in charcoal grinding, were closed about 1905. Trotter Thomas & Co. established the Cannop, or Howlers Slade, foundry in 1835, offering to supply tram plates to the S & W in 1836. The little foundry was served by sidings with a triangular junction to the branch. These had been removed by 1901, but the foundry, rebuilt in 1874, was in use until 1960. The branch fell derelict about 1920 but the track was not removed until January 1941.

The WIMBERRY SLADE branch, one mile long, ran in tree-clothed seclusion in a dry valley, with no road or even stream to keep it company. The Parliamentary plan indicates a terminus near Wimberry colliery, but the line was extended to serve other pits, and completed at about the same time as the main system. In 1868 the

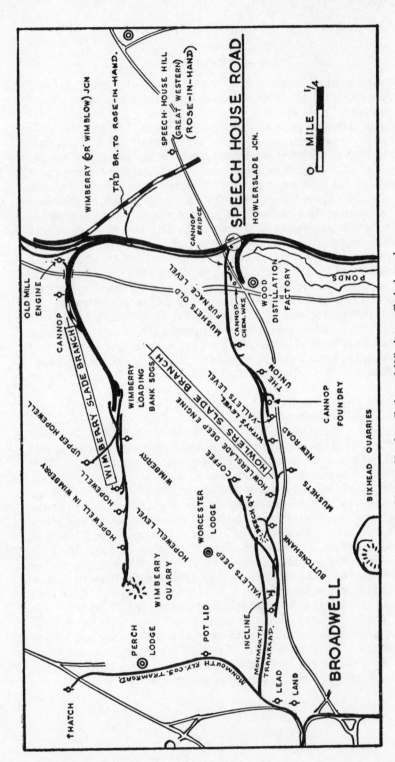

Map No. 3. Howlers Slade and Wimberry Slade branches

broad-gauge railway was laid as far as Wimberry colliery and took coal for the South Wales line, whilst the tramroad continued to handle it to Lydney Harbour.[11] The Commissioners authorised abandonment in January 1874 but the western section continued to flourish, terminating on a wharf at Hopewell Sidings, where a turntable and a winch (inscribed 'Hewlett. 1828') were used to load coal into railway wagons. An agreement was completed as late as December 1928 with Mr A. W. Brown for the use of a siding from the Wimberry tramroad, and in 1939 part of the line was still occasionally used. By February 1940, 14 chains had been taken up for repairing the Bicslade line.

In the fourteenth century the Forest miners served the King at the Berwick sieges, probably the first Army 'Sapper' unit. In 1943 their descendants, the Royal Engineers, working over the remaining 38 chains of the Wimberry line in military tractors, completely wrecked it, and it was removed entirely in 1946.

NORTH OF MIERYSTOCK

The 1½-mile-long CHURCHWAY branch had an unpromising beginning, in contrast to its later usefulness. In November 1810 Morgan was directed to extend the tramroad at Churchway to the 'engine pit', and in December, Morse of Lydbrook was authorised to use part of the branch to the turnpike at Mierystock, Morgan being told to put the line in order as soon as Morse's wagons were ready. Sheasby was instructed to complete the branch within the time limit (June 1812) in April 1812.

Rennie had suggested that a connection should be made at Churchway, preferably by the Bullo Pill line. The S & W Act fixed a rate of three-quarters the normal for coal from beyond Churchway, but this idea did not appeal to the company, and, therefore, no connection was made by either side. In 1814 the 'apparently useless' rails were taken up at Churchway and it was decided to obtain counsel's opinion whether the Bullo Pill Railway had the right to join its line. The BPR clerk protested about the lifted track but Sheasby informed him that they considered themselves justified —and proceeded to lift more plates, to complete turn-outs on the Bishopswood line.

The branch was thus moribund, but the coal-owners objected and in 1819, in response to a High Court writ of mandamus, the company resolved that Sheasby should immediately relay the line, but it would resist the proposed junction. By February 1820

Sheasby had put up a 'terminating rail and block' inscribed 'Termination of the Severn and Wye Railway at the Summit'—but this was not the final word. In 1821 an unnamed trader was repeatedly laying a connection at Churchway. Each time it was 'thrown off' by Sheasby's orders 'yet they persist in laying down the same in a temporary manner so as to force a junction', and the BPR was preparing legal action to make a connection (it advertised in November 1820 that it would supply its Lydbrook wharf with coal by road from Bilson). Finally, in January 1822, the S & W agreed that the junction 'will not operate as an act of injustice towards the miners' on its line (by letting cheap-rate coal through), its Act of 1822 repealed the cheap rate, and the BPR secured a licence for the connection, a mere 45 yd long, which was made in 1823.

After the re-establishment of ironworks at Parkend (1826) and Cinderford (1829), a traffic in ore developed from the east side of the Forest to the west, and *vice versa*, apparently with no difficulty due to gauge at the time. The western ore embodied more limestone, and a mixture produced excellent iron. In 1846 Thomas Bennett built short branches from his Nelson and Never Fear collieries to the S & W near Churchway and to the Bullo Pill line, and in 1859 he was making 'a new branch' from Nelson to the S & W. The Strip-and-at-It pit, surely the most descriptive title even in the Forest's eloquent collection, was served by two sidings. In 1841 the coal was going to Bullo Pill for country sale. Coal-raising ceased in 1861, but the works were later used by Trafalgar colliery.

In 1847 iron ore was being brought about six miles over the S & W, thence by the Forest of Dean Railway (formerly BPR) to Cinderford ironworks, but these had sent no return traffic to Lydbrook since about 1840, it being cheaper to forward some 1,200-1,500 tons annually (probably bar iron for Lydbrook works) from Churchway by road.

The FODR broad-gauge line to Churchway was opened in 1854, the tramroad being retained down to Cinderford ironworks for the east-west ore traffic, probably until 1867, when the S & W special committee visited Churchway to inspect 'the means for transferring certain traffic'. Soon after the S & W railway to Bilson Jcn was opened, in 1873, a dispute arose with the GWR and it was said that the junction was constructed 'in substitution of the transfer sidings that existed for many years near Churchway'[12]; the loaded trams were transferred by turntable on to flat wagons, for transit to Cinderford ironworks.[13] This ore traffic probably continued until

November 1875, when it began to use the railway.

The Commissioners authorised abandonment of the Churchway line in April 1877, and by the end of the month the plates had been sold. It was proposed without success in 1880 to lay a railway on the branch, to serve New Bowson and Hawkwell collieries, and Hawkwell tinplate works.

At Mierystock the junction was obscured by later sidings, but at a fence the course can be picked up, with numerous blocks, passing through wooded country for most of the way on a gently-rising gradient—Mr Morris was told that horses frequently returned to Mierystock as 'passengers' in the wagons. Plans of 1852 show two passing loops, and three tracks at Churchway, these converging again to continue as the FODR.

The MIERYSTOCK—LYDBROOK section, some 2¼ miles long, conceived as part of the main line, was severely handicapped by the difficult navigation of the Wye, described as 'in winter, a bustling, hurrying torrent, in summer a broad rivulet lounging carelessly through a rocky ravine'.[14] This was to be the northern outlet for the tramroad.

The company soon decided upon a mile-long extension to BISHOPSWOOD, falling on reasonable gradients to the riverside, thus avoiding Lydbrook incline and serving Bishopswood ironworks. This was authorised by the Act of 1810, but in August the committee advised against it, finding 'no inducement'. William Vaughan questioned the company's right to take his land in Timm's Wood without consent, but this was confirmed by the Act of 1811, provided compensation was paid.

Shortage of money for the extension, and the fact that Lydbrook was a well-established shipping place, compelled the building of the Lydbrook incline, although a 'horse road' was considered as an alternative. In August 1811 Sheasby started work but was delayed pending agreement for the use of land with Dr Symonds of Hereford, who later purchased S & W rails for use on the wharves. The committee fixed hours of working in August 1812, following a complaint, at 5 a.m. until 8 p.m. in summer, reduced at other seasons, and the 'machine and incline plane keeper' was Joseph Kings, succeeded by James Graham in 1819. The incline was self-acting, descending wagons hauling up the empty ones.

In July 1812 barge owners in the Hereford trade urged completion of the 'road to Bishopswood', but it was not until March 1814 that Sheasby was instructed accordingly, and in April he was authorised to charge half tonnage on bar iron going to Bishopswood ironworks from Lydney, and two-thirds on coal to W. Partridge, doubtless because the line was incomplete. Vaughan challenged the s & w's right to cross the road at Bishopswood, and in May he was told that it had no doubt of its powers and required him to make a wharf immediately. September saw the line at Bishopswood 'stopped' by the parish road surveyor of Walford, Herefordshire, for reasons not stated (possibly the line was being laid across the 'Bishop's Bridge' which, it may be assumed, was unsuitable)[15], and in December Sheasby was completing passing loops.

Nearing the terminus the tramroad forked, one line (of about 200 yd) crossing the road, to Bishopswood Wharf, while the other (of about 400 yd) dropped below the road and curved under it, by a short tunnel, to Cinderhill Wharf.

There were many signs that traffic to the Wye was not flourishing. In April 1816 the s & w 'leased the rates' upon all coal and goods to and from the Lydbrook and Bishopswood works to a Mr Stokes, for £420 p.a. for three years. In 1820 the company was requested to raise and repair the tramroad where it crossed the turnpike near Bishopswood, which suggests that Bishopswood Wharf was little used, and in 1821 John Partridge, building a road to his new Bishopswood house, had the rails taken up near his gate and others substituted, 'better calculated for the road', without permission. The committee was unconcerned and only rebuked Partridge in 1823, after a row between his steward, Pewtner, and Sheasby. Clearly the tramroad to the Cinderhill Wharf was also disused, or nearly so.

In 1828 Partridge proposed that the tramroad to Cinderhill Wharf be removed and the tramroad turning off near Pewtner's garden to James Ward's house (see later) become the s & w line, Partridge allocating ground for a public wharf there. The company agreed, without prejudice to its right to a wharf at Bishopswood. Similarly, the branch to Bishopswood Wharf was removed in the period 1830-1833, at Partridge's request, and the tramroad then terminated by the roadside, but no wharf was provided there, and probably no traffic was offered, for in December 1836 the drawback on coal to Bishopswood, granted in 1830 ostensibly to reduce its price in Hereford (20s 6d per ton) but more likely to counteract competition from the Abergavenny—Hereford tramroad (opened in 1829), was withdrawn.

Lydbrook, on the other hand, appears to have been enjoying some trade, for an account of 1840 described the wharf 'with little vessels lying near it, boats passing and repassing, horses, carts, men, women and children stirring along the banks'.[16]

The committee visited its northern outpost in the company's carriage in 1850, inspected 'the locality of the wharves' with Partridge, and decided that he was bound to provide a wharf at the existing terminus—probably 'Wyelands' wharf had closed, and there was no convenient means of loading from the tramroad on to road carts. Nothing transpired, however, although John Smart was granted a drawback on stone from Lydbrook to Bishopswood, to encourage a new traffic.

Lydbrook incline was shown on plans of 1853, but plans of 1856 show it as 'disused', the opening of the Hereford & Gloucester Canal (1845), the Newport, Abergavenny & Hereford Railway (1854), and the Hereford, Ross & Gloucester Railway (1855) all having affected the Wye traffic adversely. Some coal was still being carried to Bishopswood and thence by road to Ross and Hereford in 1858, but in the following year an enquirer was adroitly referred to Partridge for details of the 'wharf' at Bishopswood.

Early in 1869 G. B. Keeling stated that 'the traffic to the Wye has ceased'[17], and H. R. Lückes, who wanted to send coal from Speech House colliery to Ross, transferring it to the turnpike at Bishopswood, was told that this would necessitate re-laying a large part of the line from Mierystock. The plates and blocks were removed between Lower Lydbrook and Bishopswood in 1874, but the land was retained 'for the present'—until 1920 in fact, when it was sold.

The BISHOPSWOOD IRONWORKS had long been a feature of the Wye scene, two furnaces being in operation in the district by 1602. In August 1809 the S & W proposed to Partridge, the owner, the construction of an inclined plane up to the ironworks, and this is shown on Bryant's map (1823-1824) as an 'iron rail road' up to the forge—by 1814 smelting had ceased, bar iron being brought from Lydney. In 1816 Sheasby seized by distress 'Finers Metal' from the Bishops Wood Company, and the works probably closed in 1817. The incline apparently joined the S & W before it passed under the road, to reach Cinderhill Wharf, which owed its name to the adjacent slag dump. A stone bridge survives near the forge.

The LYDNEY TRADING SOCIETY was begun in 1821 by Samuel Holder and James Ward, who established a goods and passenger service from the Severn to the Wye, the S & W reducing rates by way of encouragement on iron, tin-plate, sand, flour, grain and grocery. A siding was built across the road near Bishopswood, to a wharf at the house now called 'Wyelands'. A rate of 2s each way until October, and afterwards 3s, was fixed for 'a Pleasure Tram

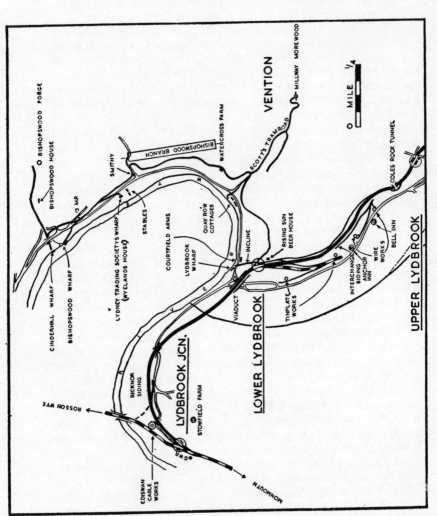

Map No. 4. Lydbrook and Bishopswood

drawn by one horse with liberty to take goods and parcels'. The 3s rate for 'all Pleasure Trams' was renewed and in 1825 achieved the status of a bye-law. Any travellers landing at Wyelands may have found hospitality at a small inn, reputed locally to have existed there.

In 1840 Sheasby was charging reduced rates because of the long journey to Bishopswood, but in 1842 Ward sought a further drawback for the weekly Ross to Bristol service via Lydney, as carriers via Gloucester, at 3s 4d per ton cheaper, had taken much of the Society's traffic. The concession was not granted and evidently the wharf soon closed, but the concern continued long active at Lydney.

SCOTT'S TRAMROAD served the Millway Moorwood level, leased by E. J. Scott from a free miner in 1817.[18] He obtained a licence for the 102 yd of line within the Forest boundary in January 1820, and set about building an 'incline plane' down to the Wye, about half-a-mile long. The s & w complained that his object was to infringe its Parliamentary rights by avoiding its line, because it refused to quote him a low toll for the short haul, its Act fixing certain rates regardless of distance so that all colliers would compete on equal terms. In 1822 Scott, a solicitor of the Poultry, was suing Sheasby for 'removing the obstruction of movable rails thrown across their railway'. A counter-action, indicting Scott for a nuisance in laying his line upon the public highway, caused his action to be dropped, but he persisted in using his line until in May 1823 the company ordered his rails to be removed where they crossed the public highways, and no more was heard of the line, which ran down the steep Ventions Lane to the roadside, and probably crossed to a wharf in front of cottages known as Quay Row. Keeling proposed to use Scott's primitive method as late as 1869, for crossing the line to New Fancy colliery with 'shifting rails' or a 'flying rail', and it was in fact used where the Howlers Slade branch crossed the Wood Distillation siding, in 1917.

The LYDBROOK IRONWORKS existed in Elizabethan times. In 1806 Thomas Allaway erected a tinplate works, leasing the nearby Lower works in 1817, and is believed to have produced the first tinplates in this country.[19] Materials came in by the tramroad, but the tinplate was shipped at Lydbrook for Bristol. The works were rented in 1871 by Richard Thomas, who formed Richard Thomas & Co. on 1 April and set up home at 'The Poplars' nearby. The old tinplate mills were dismantled after the McKinley Tariff (1890) limited trade with the U.S.A. and the works ceased operation in 1925, being dismantled in 1930.

Already old, the upper works were purchased in 1818 by the Russell family, and by 1858 comprised a forge and wireworks, making mainly telegraph and fencing wire. A tramroad connected them to the forge and an incline led to the S & W. When the railway was built, the incline was diverted to an exchange siding. The horses, which were stabled at the Anchor Inn, usually hauled two trams of wire up to the railway per trip. Russell's works were closed between 1880 and 1900.

At Mierystock the course, after crossing the main road, proceeds on a rock-strewn ledge and is soon above the site of Waterloo colliery, sunk in 1841. Before production began the pit failed; it was revived as the Arthur & Edward, an inclined plane up to the S & W, with engine house, being built in 1855; but by 1857 the pit was flooded again.

The course is now high above the Greathough Brook, in woods on Barnedge Hill. The valley is crossed by the railway embankment and the tramroad runs alongside, then passes beneath it, turning sharply to run in the opposite direction in thick woods. The brook is crossed on an embankment, followed by a turn under the railway, beside which it runs through a copse on the site of Waterloo sidings. Beyond Upper Lydbrook station the course passes round Coles rock tunnel, then crosses the railway, which falls gradually below the tramroad until they part company at Lower Lydbrook; the hillside course can be followed past the junctions with the wireworks and tinworks tramroad inclines. At Lower Lydbrook an old cottage on the left is believed to have been the S & W weigh-house, and the heavily-overgrown incline can be seen, its memory perpetuated by the 'Incline Cottages' at its top. At its foot, no signs of the wharf remain as the riverside was used for tipping many years ago.

Above Lower Lydbrook the course makes a hairpin bend, to continue as the Bishopswood branch. The tramroad follows the curving hillside for the next half-mile, affording fine panoramas of the river, the formation being buttressed by stone retaining walls on this section; the Bishopswood line is remarkable for its careful construction but it hardly lived up to expectations. Until about the end of 1951 the route from Ventions Lane was used under toll for supplying Incline Cottages with coal by horse-drawn road carts.

The sinuous formation on the hillsides can be followed with ease across Ventions Lane, through Timm's Wood, by Waterscross Farm, and across Ragman's Slade until it curves behind and above a smithy, still descending, to join the road. The 13th milepost, dated 1814, stood at this point until 1952. Large stone blocks in the water mark the site of Bishopswood wharf. The road to Nailbridge (made in 1841) obliterated part of the Cinderhill route but the tunnel under the road survives. It is stone-lined, about 9 ft high and of similar width—practically the same as Mierystock tramroad tunnel; in its south wall, beneath the road, is a deep chamber, possibly a store or toll office. Cinderhill wharf is marked by a fragment of stone facing in the river bank.

CHAPTER 5

The Severn & Wye in Disgrace (1840-1867)

THE FIRST BROADSIDE

The tramroads were fighting even before 1830 against the incursion of the steam railway, in the form of the Purton scheme. Twenty years later the conversion of the FODR had been decided upon, but converting the many miles of steep and tortuous S & W tramroads would have eaten into dividends. The company therefore clung to the old methods, making only grudging concessions to public opinion, and this intransigence produced harsh criticism from the Crown, other railway companies, and the traders.

Edward Protheroe was a man of property, a former chairman of the S & W (he resigned in 1827), and an industrialist. He told the Dean Forest Commissioners in 1832 that in 1809 or 1810 he had been asked by his uncle, John, to take some S & W shares. He took twenty £50 shares, 'but as subscribers could not be found to complete the undertaking, I gradually increased my number, as money was required, until I held 1,500 shares, nearly half the concern'.

In 1840 Protheroe wrote to Joseph Cookson, chairman of the S & W, as a mine-owner and not as chairman of the FODR. He did not suggest a fusion of the two companies, nor an extension of 'old fashioned tram plates'; to compete with Welsh coal they had to have modern railways, and he required a better, cheaper outlet for his New Fancy pits. He proposed that the S & W should extend the 'new line of Steam Carriage road' from the harbour to Foxes Bridge;* if it rejected the line, he would turn to the FODR and if that company declined, others would eagerly seize the opportunity. Cookson replied that he could not put the matter before his proprietors immediately as there was much other business, it involved heavy expense, and the coal proprietors had not supported the Grange Pill scheme; 'You will have the kindness to consider this without reference to my position with the Company'.

* The S & W does not in fact appear to have been contemplating any conversion to a steam railway at this time.

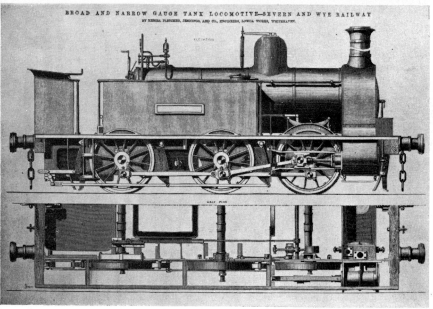

BROAD-GAUGE LOCOMOTIVES

(16) 'Forester' after conversion from tramroad use
(17) 'Robin Hood' as built for broad gauge, but readily convertible to
standard gauge

ENGINES AT WORK

(18) 'Friar Tuck' in s & w livery, at Berkeley Road

(19) 'Little John' the first, as an inspection engine; the central seated figure
is G. W. Keeling

From Hill House, Newnham, on 7 December, came thunderous reply. Protheroe had written to Cookson as chairman, and he would have to treat the reply in that light. 'I believe there is but one feeling of dissatisfaction . . . at the miserable and expensive conveyance and the petty vexation wantonly adopted by your chief officer' (i.e., Sheasby. The wheel-tread question was causing much ill-feeling). Of Grange Pill he said:

> Had you condescended to ask my opinion (and I believe that half your trade is in my hands) I should have begged you not to throw away your money in such an extravagant scheme while so many real improvements demanded attention, but ever since the management has been left to a servant the accommodation of the traders appears to have been considered a very secondary object. I do not attribute this neglect to the gentlemen who come over from Bristol to Lydney twice in the year and return the same day. They . . . like many other great bodies, find it easiest to believe and act upon all that is told them by their clerk. It is however become quite insupportable and we must try to take better care of our own interests. . . . After all, you may be assured that nothing on my part shall be done in a spirit of hostility towards a Company with whom I was so long and so cordially connected. . . . Edward Protheroe.

It is clear that had Protheroe still controlled the company its policy would have moved more with the times.

The Kidnall's Mill branch was soon put in hand, but advanced with painful slowness, and the seeds sown in 1840 eventually produced the ill-starred Central line. In October 1842 there was no dividend, owing to the outlay for new works, and the non-payment of over £2,000 from the Park End Coal Co., controlled by Protheroe and working his collieries.

The Dean Forest Mines Act (1838) produced a profound change in the organisation and scale of Forest industry. The mines had long been in a chaotic state, with ill-defined claims, so that miners sometimes met—and fought—underground. The Act established Mining Commissioners to regulate the workings and by 1846, 193 coal and iron mines, and 315 stone quarries, had been defined, and assigned to claimants who, their rights assured, began to develop their works. The need for improved transport became even more marked.

A POWERFUL OPPONENT

The proposals for the South Wales Railway were well advanced by 1844, and there was local talk that it proposed to purchase the s & w if the price was reasonable, and if not, to lay a parallel

E

railway. In 1846 the SWR was seeking powers to extend its line from Chepstow to Gloucester, to purchase and reconstruct the FODR tramroad, and to build a line from Lydney Harbour along the S & W to Teague's Bridge, near Churchway Engine, with a branch *via* Moseley Green to the FOD line at Holly Hill Inclosure. There followed a determined attempt by the S & W to sell its tramroads. On 15 January 1846 a S & W deputation headed by Cookson was received at Paddington, but on the 28th the SWR board resolved, after considering the cost of improvements and the reduction of tolls to a competitive level, that the price was too high. In May the

BYE LAW,

Made at a General Assembly of the Severn and Wye Railway and Canal Company of Proprietors, the 8th day of October, 1839.

That from and after the 1st day of October, 1840, no Hallier or other Person having the care of any Tram Waggon or Tram Waggons using the Tram Road belonging to this Company, or any part thereof, shall use any Wheel of such Tram Waggon being less upon the Rim bearing than seven-eighths of an Inch---And that each Person offending against this Rule, shall forfeit and pay to the said Company any Sum not exceeding Forty Shillings, nor less than Ten Shillings for each offence.

Commons committee proposed that, prior to the purchase of the FOD line, the SWR should also purchase the S & W. The SWR board resolved to strike out the clauses for the purchase of the FOD line unless the proviso was dispensed with; no compromise could be reached, and this was done.[1]

In 1847 the SWR again submitted a bill for purchase of the FOD line, and the S & W opposed it, claiming that the conversion to a broad-gauge railway would make interchange at Churchway difficult. The SWR still refused to purchase the S & W saying that it would lose heavily on the FODR transaction, and did not want to repeat it. It did agree, at the suggestion of the Lords committee, to contribute £15,000 towards the improvement of the s & w, to be expended under the direction of its own engineer, and obtained its Act. An indenture of 21 October 1847, covering the monetary arrangement, expressly stated that s & w traffic to Lydney should not be impeded. In the same month the s & w board authorised a strong-room for books and papers—it is irresistible to suppose that as the swr contribution was by far the biggest windfall it had enjoyed, it was determined to guard the document against all comers!

THE ATTITUDE OF THE CROWN

Evidence taken before a Commons committee on Woods and Forests in 1848 shows how resentment against the s & w tramroads was hardening; 'they can charge enormously if they choose'—Low Delph coal tonnage was 1s 6d per ton for 5 miles, plus haulage cost, and the Act allowed a charge of 3s. The s & w was paying about 8 per cent on its capital. John Buddle of Wallsend, a Mining Commissioner, told the lessee of the Parkend collieries, 'Mr. Nicholson, it is impossible things can remain as they are—you will be sure to have a railway communication', and another industrialist, Teague, joined Nicholson in urging branches from the main South Wales line.

The Commissioners of Woods and Forests in their 27th Report, 1850, again emphasised that the tolls charged were very high compared with locomotive lines and attributed the depression of 1849 in the Forest chiefly to 'this very inferior and expensive system' precluding competition with other coal districts. The s & w proposed to lower tolls by 20 per cent for two years, if its Crown rent was waived during that period, and the Commissioners agreed, hoping that during that time railways would be introduced. Income for the half-year ending 31 March 1851 was £5,195 and expenditure was £1,433.

The swr (Gloucester & dfr) was opened from Grange Court to Chepstow on 19 September 1851, and interchange facilities were soon put in at Lydney, emphasising even more the 'ancient and modern' styles. The swr was built to the gwr broad gauge, 7 ft 0¼ in. as against the standard 4 ft 8½ in. gauge of most other railways, and any track joining the swr had therefore to be broad. Blackwell, a Bristol engineer, had become consultant to the s & w, but in October 1851, after seeing his plans for improving the system, the committee hesitated to apply to Parliament 'in view of the appointment of a new Chief Commissioner' (T. F. Kennedy).

In February 1852 the chairman wrote to Kennedy that they had not deposited plans because in view of the FOD Central's approach it would have been 'indecorous'—and there were also pecuniary difficulties.[2] The Central bill seemed to contain 'such flagrant violations' of standing orders as to preclude its success, and the s & w intended to put forward plans (including a branch to Foxes Bridge, largely on Central territory). The Commissioners, undeceived by this procrastination, agreed that improvements were very desirable but asked for a bill to consider, refusing as pointless any 'desultory conversation'. The company replied that this was an unexpected discouragement, but on 23 April appointed a special committee to consider Blackwell's survey, which would have largely ante-dated the modernisation of the '70s by 20 years. The dock was to be deepened and single-line broad-gauge railways were to join the swr at Lydney, Soudley and Churchway, the Churchway branch being re-aligned to the north. The line to Lydbrook was also to be converted, but this was dropped, in view of the difficult route, the cost of a stationary engine for the incline, and the small traffic. The Moseley Green branch was to be re-aligned and extended to Foxes Bridge, with branches to Lightmoor and Soudley.

A circular was sent to traders, the Commissioners, and the swr in May urging traders to form a committee to discuss the proposals. The only reply was from Edward Protheroe, but the company declined to meet him alone. The Commissioners replied from Whitehall, setting down the conditions for their approval—'this formidable list of authoritative requisitions', the special committee called it.

(1) Part of the s & w to be converted to broad gauge, to avoid transhipment.
(2) The s & w gradients and curves to be improved.
(3) An independent Central line to be built.
(4) The s & w to offer no opposition to (3).
(5) s & w rates to be the same as the Commissioners should require on a Central line.

The Commissioners offered to receive a s & w deputation, but the company declined, stating vehemently that the coalfield was not big enough for three companies, the FODR and itself could be made adequate, and on no other basis could it consider the expenditure required. The history of the Central line amply confirms these views.

Kennedy commented in August 1852 that the Forest trade did not benefit much from the swr, as 'a tramway is a very inferior mode of conveyance, and the minerals must change waggons at Lydney, by which their quality is greatly injured'.[3]

THE COMPANY'S DECISION

With such scant support, the special committee decided not to alter the gauge or form of the line, and on 22 October the shareholders approved the following proposals:

(1) Improvement of curves and gradients; use of wrought-iron plates instead of cast-iron.

(2) Completion of the licensed line from Moseley Green to Foxes Bridge as a combined tramroad and broad-gauge railway, with a 1½-mile tramroad branch to Lightmoor (the committee had been encouraged to believe, at Paddington, that the SWR would co-operate by building a 2½-mile railway from Moseley Green to the FODR at Scilly Point, near Soudley).

(3) Increase in size of locks and basin, with a broad-gauge line from the SWR to the pier, for shipping coal from the FODR.

(4) Reduction of maximum tolls, the company to become carriers, and to use locomotives.

All this was to have cost some £68,600 plus £14,000 of the SWR money then unspent. The traders would not need to replace their wagons, capital outlay would be light, and the need for a Central line would be met; the traders had evinced no interest in broad-gauge conversion and would probably oppose tolls fixed on a rate per mile without regard to the two kinds of Delph coal (coal from the High Delph measures was of low grade, and only paid half toll —an instance was Arthur & Edward colliery).

A public meeting was held on 12 November at the Angel Inn, Coleford, on the evergreen subject of improved railways. No S & W representative was present, and the Deputy Gavellers reported to Kennedy that the meeting had condemned the alterations proposed as totally inadequate, and advocated a broad or mixed-gauge line from the SWR branch to the western boundary of the Forest. Resolutions were passed regretting the delay in providing railways, and supporting the Dean Forest, Monmouth, Usk & Pontypool Railway, and the Hereford, Ross & Gloucester Railway proposed line from Ross to Monmouth, with a branch to Lydbrook and Churchway. (The former never got much nearer the Forest than Monmouth, and the Churchway branch was not authorised.)

THE ACT OF 1853

Preparations were made to introduce the economy scheme as a bill. The special committee decided to deposit Blackwell's comprehensive plans[4], so that if further support was forthcoming it could undertake the broad gauge. Letters solicited the anticipated SWR support—'It is far from our desire to become again opponents to you'—but the SWR had deposited its Monmouth line bill, which included a branch from Scilly Point to Foxes Bridge, and moreover supported the DF, M, U & PR bill for a line from Pontypool to Coleford and the SWR at Awre, with a branch to Foxes Bridge. Saunders (the SWR secretary) wrote that provided there was no opposition to its bill, the company would agree to the S & W tramroads to Foxes Bridge and Lightmoor, but the SWR should make and work the broad-gauge line to Foxes Bridge, for economy and efficiency. The S & W, unmoved by this generosity, announced intention to retain its scheme and to oppose the other bills.

A further attempt to win over the Chief Commissioner produced scant comfort; he would, he said, have to recommend against the bill 'on the ground that the principle of levying the tonnages is objectionable and on other grounds . . . the Commissioners' objections to the bill are insuperable'.

In Parliament, the S & W opposed, and was opposed by, the SWR and DF, M, U & PR interests, the SWR opposition being withdrawn after an agreement to drop the Foxes Bridge broad-gauge line in return for SWR acquiescence in the Lightmoor branch. The Usk line opposition continued, and it failed to obtain powers east of Coleford. The Commissioner compelled the S & W to strike out all clauses involving Crown lands, including the doubling of track from Parkend to Mierystock to reduce wear on plates and trams, the Lightmoor branch, and a permanent grant of the line from Phelps Meadow to Foxes Bridge.

The Act was secured on 15 August 1853[5], and the special committee reported it on 21 October as a great success, saying that it was only the Chief Commissioner's opposition which prevented it obtaining the full authority sought, and adding with some satisfaction that he had not advanced his own purpose of a central line. The company was authorised to become carriers, to let out trams for hire, to purchase locomotives, and to make minor deviations between Lydney Jcn and Lydney Town, between Upper Forge and Tufts, and on the Kidnall's Mill branch near Tufts. A capital issue of £30,000 in £20 shares was permitted, existing capital consisting of 3,762 shares of £50 each. (In April 1853 a dividend of 20s per share, free of income tax, had been declared.)

The Act also enabled the company to purchase the Bathurst wharfs, and this was done for a fixed payment in perpetuity of £650 p.a. The original maximum tolls of 3s and 1s 6d per ton were reduced to 1s 3d and 10d respectively, and power was given to reduce charges for through traffic to the SWR. The committee welcomed this as 'a point of somewhat minor value', for their opponents could no longer quote extravagant tolls which were never levied.

It is hardly surprising that locomotives were not introduced for many years, as it must have been obvious that their use on the tramroad was far from ideal. The S & W proceeded at leisurely pace with the meagre improvements authorised. In February 1857 the lower part of the line and the Lydney interchange were being improved, the cost being partly met by the SWR. The £15,000 was being spent, but hardly as the reluctant donors had anticipated—no S & W broad gauge was to appear for another decade, and small wonder that in April 1858 Brunel, the SWR and GWR engineer, was unable to meet the directors at Lydney to inspect the 'new works'.

Joseph Cookson was chairman for the last time at the general meeting on 26 October 1859, being succeeded by Odiarne C. Lane, who was followed by A. Graham Clarke in 1865. The Crown continued to urge the S & W to convert lines, use locomotives and lower tolls, but refused any financial aid, such as it gave the FOD Central Railway, which it used as a competitive spur to the S & W. Eventually, in 1864, the S & W did introduce locomotives on the tramroads, but transhipment at Lydney Jcn, and general discontent, continued.

In 1866 the board considered an offer to purchase its undertaking, made anonymously through Baxter, Rose, Norton & Co., but the price was fixed at £165,500, and this seems to have ended the 'take-over bid'. These solicitors were also acting for the FODCR, but that concern was hardly in a position to purchase anything.

An ambitious scheme was in the air to provide a standard-gauge route from South Wales to the Midlands by an extension of the Northampton & Banbury Jcn Railway to Ross, the projected Ross & Monmouth Railway, and the CMU & PR.* In 1866 its engineer recommended a branch from Stowfield to Lydbrook Church, to connect with the S & W. The Keelings told R & M representatives that

* A successor to the DF, M, U & PR, 'Coleford' being substituted for 'Dean Forest'.

they desired to convert their line to standard gauge but could not promise to apply for powers in 1867. In that year the conversion of the Bishopswood branch and its extension to join the R & MR near Kerne Bridge was suggested, but the directors, after a flying visit in the company's carriage, remained unimpressed. Another active aspirant for the South Wales traffic was the Worcester, Dean Forest & Monmouth Railway[6], authorised in 1863 against opposition from the S & W and other companies.

ECLIPSE OF THE TRAMROADS

All these grandiose schemes perished and S & W affairs dragged until, as recounted in Chapter 6, the broad-gauge railway was introduced in 1868, quickly followed by the standard gauge. Throughout this period the tramroad continued in operation down to Lydney harbour, but some of its branches were already idle or nearly so, and the railway finally rendered it superfluous.

The Commissioners consented to the abandonment of the tramroad between Speculation colliery and the Tufts on 28 January 1874 and notice was given to freighters. A dispute developed because the Wye Colliery Co. wanted the section from Speculation colliery which took coal to the pumping engine at Wimberry retained, but the S & W required the land for its railway from White Gates to Mierystock. The Commissioners allowed abandonment from Speculation to Lydbrook after the S & W agreed to leave 250 yd of tramroad from Speculation to Mierystock siding, and on 22 December 1874 agreed to abandonment of the remainder.

The tramroad south of Upper Forge, still required by Richard Thomas & Co., was east of the railway to New Mills, where it crossed over on the level, a branch to Middle Forge also crossing on the level. In 1875 the S & W laid a new tramroad from New Mills to Middle Forge, east of the railway, eliminating New Mills crossing, whilst Middle Forge crossing was controlled by a signal and ground frame. In 1876 Bathurst refused to permit the tramroad from the Tufts to Lydney Basin to be removed before the lease of his collieries expired. The tramroad across the SWR was removed in 1879, but after pleas from Richard Thomas it was agreed to leave the remainder down for six months, except at Middle Forge and other dangerous places, and between Middle Forge and New Mills it was not lifted until 1883.

CHAPTER 6

Reconstruction and Expansion (1867-1879)

THE BROAD GAUGE

The S & W directors, investigating the question of improvement once again, reported on 12 June 1867 that 'the shareholders need scarcely be reminded that their line consists of a tramway . . . until recently wholly worked by horse power . . .'; steam power had only partially met the requirements of existing traffic and material changes had taken place since 1852. The FOD line was a broad-gauge railway, the Central line was about to be opened, the Worcester, DF & Monmouth Railway was authorised on standard gauge. The traders still clamoured for a railway; John Trotter Thomas wrote that he could increase output from Wimberry Pit—'only let us out on the edge rail', he cried.

The directors advocated a temporary broad-gauge line for about eight miles from the High Delph collieries (principally Wimberry) to Lydney (GWR), costing about £12,000, and readily convertible to standard gauge; they urged application for powers to convert all or part of their tramroads to single-line mixed-gauge railways.

The company approached the Commissioners of Woods for financial aid without success, and in 1868 a Board of Trade certificate authorised a further £38,000 of capital. The company accepted offers of 75¾ lb. per yd flanged edge rails from J. W. Armstrong (GWR Hereford divisional engineer) at Carmarthen.

No time was lost in laying the broad-gauge line alongside the tramroad, largely on the east side; the majority of the tramroad branches in use went off to the west, and level crossings were thus avoided. The new line was largely on s & w-leased land, the only significant deviation on to Crown land being some 200 yd in a cutting near Whitecroft, to avoid a curve.

On 30 September 1868 the company advised freighters that the broad-gauge line was being laid, and on 11 November it was ready for traffic, the directors travelling to Wimberry Slade behind locomotive No. 5; the Commissioners, however, refused consent and the line remained idle until 'we laid the line upon our land at that point, to avoid the curve'. Traffic commenced on 19 April 1869 and included Welsh coke for Parkend furnaces, the wagons carrying 10 tons, against 2¼ tons on the tramroad. Little traffic was carried at first, the traders not having arranged with the GWR for a supply of wagons, but the s & w had two broad-gauge locomotives. The double tramroad up to Parkend, and the single line beyond, were retained.[1]

The decade from 1869 was the s & w renaissance, for the company which had instituted a system of tramroads through the Forest 60 years before, did the same with railways, albeit belatedly. The company fought its greatest Parliamentary battle in 1869, when seeking authority for the railway laid in 1868, and for the Mineral Loop line from Tufts Jcn to Wimberry Jcn, with a branch to Bilson. The FODCR bitterly opposed the Loop line and the GWR was also amongst the petitioners.

The s & w claimed that the Mineral Loop would give soft-coal pits in the east an adequate seaborne outlet; Sir Patrick Colquhoun, counsel for the FODCR, described it as a 'poaching line', since these pits already had outlets to either the Moseley Green branch, the Central line, or the GWR. Nevertheless, none of these was an efficient outlet to the Bristol channel, for Bullo Pill was inadequate, Brimspill uncompleted, and all traffic for Lydney harbour was still going over the tramroad. Trotter Thomas, owning Wimberry colliery, said that he did not use the tramroad much for supplying coal to Cinderford and Soudley ironworks, due to unsatisfactory arrangements at Churchway.[2]

The Act, dated 26 July 1869[3], confirmed the existing railway, and authorised as broad-gauge railways (to be quickly converted to any gauge adopted by the GWR) the Mineral Loop and a branch to the GWR at Bilson. Railway No. 3, dropped from the bill at the Commissioners' insistence, was to have run from a point north of Wimberry Jcn to Mierystock. The company was always to maintain continuous communication, by tramroad or railway, along the existing line and branches down to the outer harbour, and the tramroad was to be continued concurrently with the railway to link unconverted branches with the harbour (in later years, in fact, several tramroads were left high and dry on interchange wharves). Abandoned tramroad sites were to revert to the Crown, a branch was to be laid from the GWR to Lydney outer harbour within five years, at least one train was to be run each way daily, except Sundays, and the company was empowered to charge on a ton-per-mile basis on its railways.

A broad-gauge line beside the Moseley Green branch to the Compressed Coal Co.'s Pillowell level (48 chains) was completed in November 1869, and a weighbridge was placed near Lydney church-yard. Keeling was authorised to extend the broad gauge towards Moseley Green (not done), and to a new coal tip at Lydney basin.

With the decline of the Wye navigation and the development of iron-ore traffic to South Wales (the Ebbw Vale and Dowlais Iron Cos. had acquired Forest interests) the need arose for a railway outlet to the nascent Ross & Monmouth Railway, which with the Coleford, Monmouth, Usk & Pontypool Railway, provided a route to the ironworks at the heads of the Welsh valleys, free of the arduous climb from the coast.

A further Act, 12 May 1870[4], authorised a railway 4 miles 2 furlongs long, from the main line ('Whitegates Jcn'), to a triangular junction with the R & MR near Lydbrook, also a 1 mile 1 furlong railway from Serridge Jcn to the Lydbrook line ('Mierystock Jcn'). The north curve at Lydbrook was not built (although earthworks were prepared) and neither was the Whitegates Jcn line, on a similar route to railway No. 3 of 1869, but the S & W agreed in 1882 to rate Richard Thomas & Co.'s traffic as if it were, instead of by the longer route used.

Grierson, the GWR general manager, informed the S & W of the intention to convert the South Wales line, in February 1871, and it was decided to lay standard gauge on the Mineral Loop, and a third rail from Tufts Jcn to the harbour, whence the broad gauge had been extended. However, over a year was to pass before the stan-dard gauge was introduced, and several traders asked without suc-cess for railway facilities on the tramroad branches. In 1871 there were indications of a rapid development in mineral traffic, but in 1872 strikes led to a falling off; receipts were down by £1,800, but a dividend of 8s per £50 share was paid for the half year.

The S & W decided to convert the Milkwall tramroad and extend it to Coleford, also to convert and extend the Dyke branch to join the Coleford line, thus serving the Oakwood valley. The GWR promoted the Coleford Railway from Monmouth to the Oakwood valley. The S & W was again face to face with Paddington and negotiations were unsuccessful. In January 1872 the Commissioner of Woods asked for the company's views on the Coleford bill, especially the proposed continuation into the valley. G. B. Keeling replied that the Commissioner had urged them to extend to Coleford, and they had deposited plans, yet within a few days of the closing date for notices the GWR scheme was deposited, 'calculated hereafter to be continued across and to the serious detriment of our main line'; they urged him not to sanction the GWR Oakwood extension.

The Commons committee passed both bills, provided that if the Coleford Co. built its extension, the S & W should make an end-on junction with it, with running powers into a joint station at Coleford. If on the other hand the S & W did not make a line to Easter Mine within two years, the Coleford Co. could make it. In the House of Lords, the S & W did not oppose the Coleford concern, not wanting to incur GWR hostility unnecessarily. The GWR, however, entertaining no such sentiments, opposed the S & W and even got up a formidable petition, ostensibly signed by many leading traders; but Mr Lückes (who had an intimate knowledge of the Foresters, as banker and mine-owner) revealed that they included a blacksmith, a foreman, labourers, quarrymen and hauliers. The S & W was dismayed that the Lords gave the GWR running powers over all the lines authorised, instead of limiting them to the Oakwood valley, but was reasonably satisfied.

The Act of 18 July 1872[5] authorised a railway from Coleford Jcn to Coleford, the Oakwood branch from Tufts Jcn to the Oakwood chemical works, the Oakwood and Milkwall Junction railway from 'Knockley Gate Jcn' (on the Oakwood branch) to the Coleford branch near Darkhill. The Act also authorised passenger traffic. The Junction railway was never built, and the Oakwood branch was never completed. The Severn Bridge Railway Act was also passed in 1872, but this, and the far-reaching effect it had on S & W history, will be dealt with in Chapter 8.

THE BEGINNING OF DECLINE

Railway construction progressed, as described in Chapter 7; in 1875 passenger services began, and a bill for a 'Severn Bridge and Bristol Port and Channel Dock Jcn Railway' was introduced, but withdrawn. The S & W was transformed into a full-fledged railway, but the times were not easy; industrial disputes were common, competition from Spanish iron ore was being felt in the Forest, and the system was hemmed in by the GWR. In May 1876 the directors reported that little was needed to handle a large increase of traffic, but trade depression actually reduced what there was, and maintenance was unduly heavy owing to a wet season. The company created 3,000 £10 preference shares at 5 per cent, under a Board of Trade certificate, but only 191 were taken up.

In 1877 economy was still the watchword. Money for reconstruction had been lent by bankers to the directors, on personal liability, and the company had to repay it. No ordinary dividends had been paid since September 1873, and for the half-year 1874-1875 only half rates were paid on preference shares. An Act of 23 July 1877[6] extinguished the 1876 certificate and increased the authorised capital by £60,000 for discharging debts, and for improvements. The new shares were to have preference over the existing preference shares, and the holders of these petitioned against the bill. The existing capital consisted of £315,471 in shares and £104,353 on loan.

CHAPTER 7

The Severn & Wye Railways

THE MAIN LINE

This embodied the existing broad-gauge line up to Wimberry, while the section thence to Drybrook Road (technically part of the Mineral Loop), with the section to Bilson Jcn, was originally called the 'Trafalgar' or 'Cinderford' branch, being designed as a mineral route between the eastern and western valleys. The original main line was completed by the Lydbrook branch, but was extended in 1879 by the Severn Bridge Railway, in 1894 by the MR Sharpness branch (both described in Chapter 8), and in 1900 by the Cinderford extension. The 'up' direction for train working was to Berkeley Road Jcn.

By mid-June 1872 the Loop line was extended from Drybrook Road to join the existing line at Wimberry, but in February 1873 the completion of the junction at Bilson was still awaited; the GWR was never quick to provide such facilities for the S & W, and Bilson junction was not opened for traffic until 15 September. The east-west iron ore traffic did not commence until November 1875, probably due to difficulty in agreeing rates.

Meanwhile the Lydbrook extension from Serridge Jcn was delayed by non-completion of the Ross & Monmouth Railway. Richard Thomas suggested in May 1871 that 'influential parties' could make it, but the S & W would not be hurried, and the impatient industrialists promoted their own northern outlet (the abortive Mitcheldean Road & FOD Jcn Railway). J. E. Billups, the Cardiff contractor, started work in June 1872 on the S & W line, which included Mierystock tunnel, Lydbrook viaduct and formidable earthworks. A serious slip in February 1873 threatened the Waterloo flour mill, and was inspected by the directors when they walked from Mierystock to Lydbrook. On 10 May they travelled by steam to Mierystock, and thence by tram carriage to Lydbrook, where they met the R & MR directors, whose line, worked by the GWR, was opened on 4 August.

The foundation stone of the viaduct had been laid on 9 November 1872, and the Crumlin Viaduct Works Co. contracted at £7,396 for its construction, Billups carrying out the masonry work. The three wrought-iron Warren girders, two of 120-ft, and one of 150 ft, spanned masonry piers about 90 ft high. The chairman and officials attended the opening of the Lydbrook line for mineral traffic on Wednesday 26 August 1874, and rounded off the occasion by presenting G. W. Keeling with a silver salver, in recognition of his skill and ability.

Colonel Rich of the Board of Trade reported on 7 June 1875 that the two highest piers of Lydbrook viaduct showed slight settlements. He noted in August that a temporary engine shed at Upper Lydbrook required removal, to clear a site for the home signal. An engine named *Self* is said to have worked on this part of the s & w in 1874; it was probably Billups' property, and the occupant of the shed.

MAIN-LINE PASSENGER SERVICES

Colonel Rich inspected the line three times before passing it as safe for passengers on 18 September 1875; he required signalling improvements, signal cabins, station clocks, check rails on curves, shelters on both platforms at crossing stations, and the 'terminal station' at Drybrook Road to be signalled as a junction.

On Thursday 23 September 1875 the first public passenger train departed from Lydney Jcn at noon for Lydbrook Jcn, drawn by *Robin Hood* and carrying the chairman, the directors and the Keelings. Rain fell persistently; the event was signalised by the firing of cannon, but by little else. Trains reversed at Drybrook Road, and engines doubtless ran round their trains there. In October *Bradshaw* recorded five trains in each direction, two of which ran between Lydney and Parkend only, and one between Drybrook Road and Lydbrook Jcn only. The Lydney—Lydbrook journey times varied between 66 and 80 minutes. This slender service was pruned to three each way in December (the last running to and from Drybrook Road only), and in July 1879 only one ran throughout, plus a down train to Upper Lydbrook which returned from the junction, and an extra Saturdays-only train to Cinderford.

For some years, beginning in 1907, the 11.15 a.m. to Lydbrook Jcn worked through to Symonds Yat in July and August only, and in 1912 an afternoon train (Thursdays and Saturdays only) from Cinderford did likewise. Reference to the withdrawal of passenger services will be found in Chapter 9.

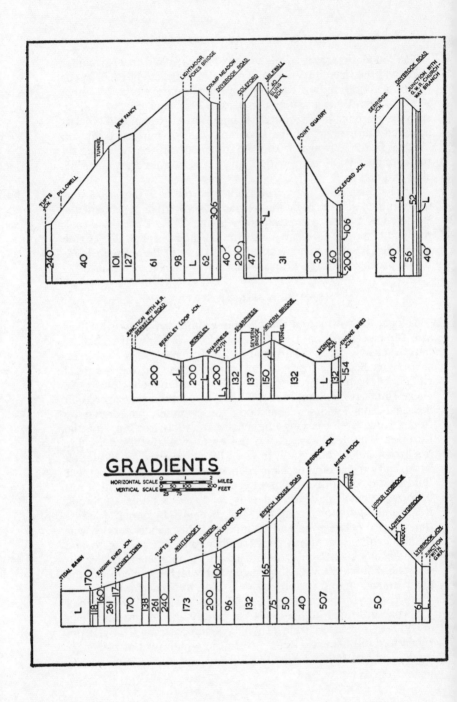

GRADIENTS

HORIZONTAL SCALE 0   1   2   MILES
VERTICAL SCALE 50   100   200   FEET
25   75

STABLE COMPANIONS

(20) 'Friar Tuck' in early standard-gauge days
(21) 'Little John' the second, as MR No. 1123A
(22) 'Severn Bridge' as built

THE MAID AND HER MAN

(23) 'Robin Hood' on standard gauge
(24) 'Maid Marian' as built, showing counter-pressure brake pipes

THE PASSENGER STATIONS

The central feature was a small timber building with gabled roof, comprising a booking office and a waiting room. The original platform and shelter at Lydney Jcn, superseded by the present station in 1879, was at right angles to the GWR up platform, the trains using a dead-end track on its east side. An access subway from the road is the only surviving relic. The S & W employed only a stationmaster there in 1875, paying the GWR £60 p.a. for passenger traffic transfer services, and it was not until 1895 that the GWR made the appalling discovery that for 16 years it had been performing the much longer 'haul' to the 1879 station under the same agreement. The other original stations were Lydney Town, Whitecroft, Parkend, Speech House Road, Drybrook Road, Upper Lydbrook and Lower Lydbrook.

At Lydney Town the original wooden buildings are on the up platform. In 1896-1897 a new building was provided, on the down platform, and the signal box there was replaced by one close to the level crossing, the original being converted into a stationmaster's office while the wooden superstructure was re-erected at Serridge Jcn. Whitecroft originally had only an up platform, the building being situated thereon. Parkend, with two platforms, was the passenger junction for Coleford and 11 men were employed there in 1904. The building, on the down platform, was removed by 1932.

Coleford Junction platform, with shelter, was provided in 1889-1890 for the workmen in David & Sant's new stoneworks, who took tickets at the signal box. The platform was removed in 1895, having become decayed, and a new one was built, but was closed in January 1906, being little used. Coleford passengers on certain trains latterly changed at the platform, instead of at Parkend, but it did not appear in the public timetables.

Speech House Road had only one platform, on the up side. Serridge platform was built for the benefit of the keeper at Serridge Lodge, and was first shown in Bradshaw in September 1878; soon only down trains called there, when the guard was advised, and it was last mentioned by Bradshaw in October 1879.

Drybrook Road was planned on the south side of the Loop line, to be named 'Nelson Road', but the platform was built on the main-line down side, and the original 'shed' becoming dilapidated, it was replaced by that from Cinderford old station in 1901, which survived until about 1954.

Although Drybrook Road was described as serving Cinderford, it

F

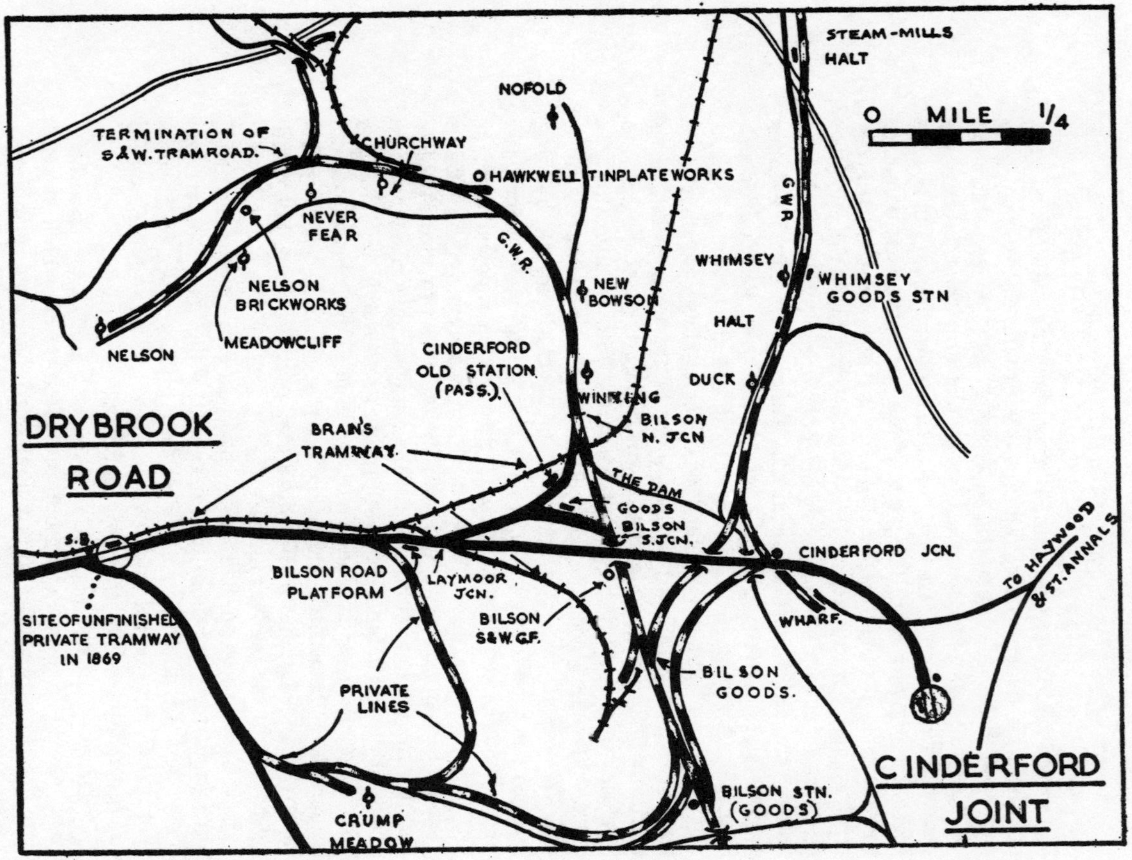

Map No. 5. Cinderford

was a mile-and-a-half from it, and Bilson platform, a temporary wooden structure with shed, was soon built about half-a-mile eastward. When Colonel Yolland inspected this 'drop platform'[1], Keeling assured him that they did not intend to take passengers across the Trafalgar tramway[2], which the s & w crossed, and agreed that it would be desirable to get rid of it before building a permanent station on a level part of the branch. He intended using only one carriage from Drybrook Road, and the Colonel insisted on a brake van, or a brake inside the coach, in case a coupling broke. The platform was sanctioned for one year, and *Engineering* for 8 September 1876 recorded that the s & w 'have opened their passenger line to Cinderford'. The Board of Trade authorised use for another year in September 1877, without further option.

Cinderford station, replacing Bilson platform, consisted of a platform with a wooden building, on the north spur at Bilson, opened on 5 August 1878. In 1880 Mr Smith of the Lion Hotel began to run an omnibus, or wagonette[3], to meet trains, at a fare of 6d to any place in Cinderford, but it lost money, and the company granted him a £20 subsidy for one year. In 1884 tradesmen were pressing for a more convenient station, but it was not until 2 July 1900 that this was opened, and the old one closed. GWR trains began to use the station in 1908 and the stationmaster, a GWR official, was instructed to be completely impartial—his cap was non-standard, lettered 'Stationmaster' without the 'GWR'.

Upper Lydbrook station has a standard wooden building (long used as a dwelling) on the up platform, a shelter on the down platform, probably added in 1892, having been removed after 1929.

Lower Lydbrook station, a single platform on the up side, was little more than an unstaffed halt, with a small shelter; from June 1880 it figured as a 'signal station' in *Bradshaw*, trains stopping to pick up passengers only when the signal was set, and it was closed on 1 April 1903.

TRAFFIC WORKING

Many sidings were restricted in layout, had inadequate shunting spurs, and were situated on severe gradients, and special instructions governed working at Norchard, Bicslade, Crown, Brierley, Waterloo (Pludds) and Bicknor, involving the placing of wagons in the rear of the brake van and backing in, use of a second van, and spragging of wheels if vehicles had to be left on the main line. There was always a long list of permanent speed restrictions, including Lydbrook viaduct (6 m.p.h., reduced to 5 in 1911), and Speculation curve (10 m.p.h., increased to 15 in 1911).

The Third, or Mineral, single line from Lydney Jcn to Lydney Town, provided in 1889 on the tramroad course, could be used by down (i.e. northbound) trains if the down line was blocked. By 1906 it was used in the morning solely for shunting and weighbridge purposes from the south end, and after 11 a.m. only for up trains.

Before the first war it was usual for the 6.18 a.m. down goods train from Lydney Jcn to consist of two engines, empty wagons for Trafalgar, Foxes Bridge and Crump Meadow collieries, and two empty coaches. Reaching Speech House Road, two trips took the stock up to Drybrook Road, whence the engines served Cinderford old station and the collieries, one then taking the coaches to Cinderford new station to work the up passenger train. A later goods train, also sometimes double-headed, served Speech House Road, the Wimberry branch, and Upper Lydbrook; these, and the other trains, were kept fully occupied serving the many sidings through the long working day.

SIGNALLING

The electric telegraph was introduced in 1874 up to Parkend, and was soon extended to Lydbrook. By 1881 the Speech House Hotel had a private wire linked in, so that 'guests may communicate with any portion of the civilised globe, without stepping out of doors'[4], and from 1887 G.P.O. telegrams were sent over the company's wires to Speech House and intermediately. Serridge Jcn signal box was made a postal telegraph office in 1888, the collieries erected telephone wires thereto, and a lengthy dispute ensued with the G.P.O. The box was closed for public message business in 1928, but the wires were still used for telegrams until Lightmoor was closed in 1940.

In 1875, in anticipation of passenger traffic, semaphore signalling was provided, and as the line was single track, train staff and ticket control (whereby a train was not permitted to enter a section unless the driver was in possession of a baton, known as a train staff, or a ticket signifying that the staff would follow) was adopted, supplemented by the block telegraph. The signal lamps were white for 'all clear' and red for 'danger', but in 1898 the white aspect was altered west of Sharpness to green, to conform with standard practice, and with the ex-MR line. The red distant lights were converted to yellow in 1945.

After 1894, signalling was a GWR responsibility until 1906, when the MR took over from Coleford Jcn and Pillowell to Berkeley Road, this in turn being transferred from London Midland Region to Western Region in 1948. The boxes south of Parkend are of MR type, except for Sharpness station and Berkeley Loop Jcn.

It was soon necessary to double the line south of Parkend; this was done from Lydney (S. Wales line crossing) to the churchyard in 1873, and thence to Lydney Town in 1874, although it was necessary to use one line for lay-by purposes until 1887, when additional sidings were provided. The Lydney Town—Tufts Jcn section was never doubled, and in 1887 Tyers electric train tablet (ETT) apparatus was installed on this bottleneck, permitting a train to enter the section at either end if clear, instead of a trip having to be made to return the train staff. The doubling of the Tufts Jcn—Whitecroft section was begun in 1891, but not completed until 1896, Whitecroft to Parkend following in 1897.

In 1889 the block sections were:

Sharpness station—Sharpness East cabin ...	Double line
(the box later known as 'Sharpness North Jcn')	
Sharpness East cabin—Severn Bridge station ...	ETT
Severn Bridge station—Lydney Jcn cabin A ...	,,
Lydney Jcn cabin A—Lydney Town	Double line
Lydney Town—Tufts Jcn	ETT
Tufts Jcn—Parkend station	,,
Parkend station—Coleford Jcn	Double line
Coleford Jcn—Speech House Road	Staff and ticket
Speech House Road—Serridge Jcn	,,
Serridge Jcn—Drybrook Road	,,
Drybrook Road—Cinderford station	Staff, one engine in steam
Serridge Jcn—Upper Lydbrook	Staff and ticket
Upper Lydbrook—Lydbrook Jcn	,,

The ETT system was in use between Coleford Jcn and Speech House Road by 1890; otherwise, all sections were still worked as above in 1894, but in 1898 the intermediate post at Traveller's Rest Crossing was made a block post, and Tyers equipment was installed between Serridge Jcn and Upper Lydbrook, while in 1903 the Station and North boxes at Sharpness were amalgamated in one box on the down platform. In 1906 the block sections were:

Berkeley Road—Berkeley Loop Jcn	Double line
Berkeley Loop Jcn—Berkeley	,,
Berkeley—Sharpness South	,,
Sharpness S—Sharpness station	,,
Sharpness station—Severn Bridge station ...	ETT No. 2, non-restoring type

Severn Bridge station—Lydney Jcn (Otters Pool)	ETT No. 2
Lydney Jcn (Otters Pool)—Lydney Engine Shed	Double line
Lydney Engine Shed—Lydney Town	,,
Lydney Town—Tufts Jcn	ETT No. 1, NRT
Tufts Jcn—Whitecroft	Double line
Whitecroft—Parkend	,,
Parkend—Travellers Rest Crossing	,,
Travellers Rest Crossing—Coleford Jcn ...	,,
Coleford Jcn—Speech House Road	ETT No. 6, restoring type
Speech House Road—Serridge Jcn	,,
Serridge Jcn—Drybrook Road	ETT No. 2, NRT
Drybrook Road—Cinderford	ETT No. 6, RT
Serridge Jcn—Upper Lydbrook	ETT No. 2, NRT (soon replaced by ETT No. 6, RT)
Upper Lydbrook—Lydbrook Jcn	Electric train staff

The Drybrook Road—Cinderford section was split into two parts, each on ETT system, in 1908, when the GWR Bilson Loop was opened to Cinderford Jcn.

The following changes were made as traffic declined:

1927. Serridge Jcn—Drybrook Road—Cinderford Jcn. Made one block section, with an intermediate token pillar instrument in Drybrook Road office, where the box was converted to a ground frame.
Cinderford Jcn—Cinderford. Train staff introduced, Cinderford box and signals taken out of use.

1929. Serridge Jcn—Upper Lydbrook—Lydbrook Jcn. Made one section, worked with a train staff, Upper Lydbrook box becoming the South ground frame (for the crossing gates), and the North ground frame being established for the points.

1930 (30 November). Tufts Jcn—Whitecroft station—Parkend station. Sections singled, combined and controlled by electric train staff, Whitecroft box being closed.

1931 (26 July). Berkeley Road—Sharpness South. The three sections singled, combined and controlled by ETT, a separate ETT system splitting the line into two sections when Berkeley Loop Jcn box was switched in. (Berkeley Loop was closed on 27 Jan 1963.)

1950 (31 December). Cinderford Jcn—Cinderford. Section merged with Bilson Jcn to Cinderford Jcn (where the box was closed).

1951 (30 April). Speech House Road—Serridge Jcn. Train staff introduced.

1951 (9 December). Speech House Road—Lydbrook Jcn. The two sections were amalgamated, and worked on the 'one engine in steam' principle, with train staff, Serridge box becoming a ground frame.

CLOSURE NORTH OF SPEECH HOUSE ROAD

From 25 July 1949 the booked freight service was withdrawn between Serridge Jcn and Cinderford Jcn, the track being broken near those points on 31 December 1950. This line was formally closed from 9 December 1951, but the section from the s & w junction at Bilson to Drybrook Road continued to be used intermittently until 1953 to clear Acorn Patch depot, and the track was not lifted until 1956, a spur being left at Serridge Jcn to give access to Mierystock.

Meanwhile closure of the Lydbrook line was often considered, but in 1951 the engine of the morning empty-wagon train to Mierystock still proceeded daily (soon curtailed to 'as required') to Lydbrook Jcn with the guards van, to pick up any wagons offered, and from 1 January 1953 it terminated at Upper Lydbrook, rarely proceeding in practice beyond Mierystock. From Monday 30 January 1956 the line from Mierystock to Lydbrook Jcn was closed, but the track remained *in situ* until 1959—1960, and a short length at Lydbrook Jcn survived as a private siding for the Ediswan works.

Mierystock sidings provided daily coal traffic until closure on 31 July 1956; the low output did not justify track renewals. Traffic was soon resumed, however, and continued until 5 August 1960. Cannop colliery was closed in September, the last traffic (scrap metal) worked out from it on 21 November, and track lifting between Mierystock and Speech House Road was completed in February 1962, an enthusiasts' special train (13 May 1961) being the last to use Serridge Jcn, apart from the demolition train.*

THE MAIN LINE DESCRIBED

Leaving Lydney Jcn station (to which point the line will be described in Chapter 8) the line curved past Lydney Yard box, picking up the West Loop before Engine Shed box (formerly Tin Works Jcn, 8 miles 32 chains from Berkeley Road), which controlled the junction of the s & w and SBR lines, the former giving access to the engine shed and Lydney tinplate works before proceeding to Lydney docks. The 'Third, or Mineral line' commences on the down side.

North of Engine Shed Jcn was a wagon-repair factory† siding and a weighbridge loop from the Third line. Pidcock's private canal runs on the up side, having passed under the line before Lydney Town

* Closures north of Parkend are referred to in Appendix 1.
† Now (1971) an engineering works.

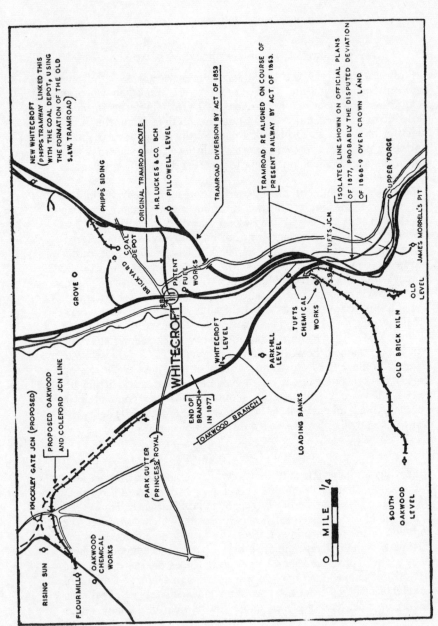

Map No. 6. Tufts Jcn and Whitecroft

station (8 miles 73 chains), behind the up platform of which was the former Lydney Foundry,* purchased by the s & w in 1856 and leased to several concerns; its siding was removed many years ago.

Beyond the level crossing the line becomes single, three sidings serving a coal depot. The old canal, the Cannop Brook and a road follow the line on the up side, through the pleasant woods which form the typical lineside scene henceforward. On the up side was Norchard siding, which served Norchard colliery and the West Gloucester power station,* established in 1923 and latterly supplied with Pillowell coal. The South connection was removed in 1948, and the siding in 1959. To the north is the site of an earlier siding which, with a tramroad exchange siding, was provided in 1873 to serve Norchard level and New Mills.

The line keeps to the shallow but pleasing valley of the Cannop Brook, or Lyd, and at Tufts Jcn the Oakwood branch diverged (10 miles 54 chains) in front of the signal box, and 6 chains beyond, the Mineral Loop diverged. Northward, on the down side, were two sidings laid by the Tytherington Stone Co. in 1939, to load crushed slag for road making.

Whitecroft station (11 miles 21 chains) had a siding and goods shed behind the down platform, and a level crossing, beyond which the line soon enters thick forest with the road and brook on the down side; the track doubles before entering Parkend station. From a loop behind the down platform here, a branch crosses two roads to Parkend Goods, formerly Parkend Marsh Sidings—three sidings in front of a wharf, on which the Oakwood tramroad terminated.

North of Parkend level crossing, beyond which the track has been lifted, the ironworks engine house survives, but nothing of the tinplate works, which had their own siding. Between Travellers Rest crossing and Coleford Jcn (12 miles 71 chains) the track continued double, with several long sidings. Parkend was a natural centre for stone works; Payne & Townsend's was established by 1870 but the siding connection, long disused, was removed in 1911. In 1889 David & Co. erected stone sawmills, with a siding, using a locomotive crane built by Booth Bros. The concern became part of the United Stone Firms Ltd. and Parkend works was closed in 1932.

Leaving Coleford Jcn the line became single and ran for nearly a mile to Bicslade siding, latterly little used. It was sometimes necessary, when shunting here, to resort to 'tow-roping', and a north connection was added in 1902. The line passed Cannop Ponds and became double before Speech House Road station (14 miles 67

* Now (1971) demolished.

chains). Sidings served the former tramroad wharf, the wood distillation works (built in 1917), and a goods shed and wharf. Beyond
the level crossing the original line was single, and at Wimberry
Jcn a branch proceeded to the loading bank serving the Wimberry
Slade tramroad. In 1912, to serve the new Cannop colliery, the
Wimberry branch was extended parallel to the main line, to enable
coal trains to run direct to Speech House Road, with a scissors crossing north of the station, and sidings between the two running lines.

On the up side a half-mile branch to Speech House Hill (later
Great Western) colliery was laid jointly by the s & w and the
colliery in 1874. The colliery was disused by 1906, the track being
removed in 1914—1915, but the pit was retained as an emergency
exit for Lightmoor.

The route curves on an embankment through the forest, over the
Cannop Brook, with glimpses of the Lydbrook line at a higher level.
Approaching Serridge Jcn (16 miles 33 chains), Crown siding passed
through a gate, to a small wharf; laid in 1903 for loading Crown
timber, it fell out of use about 1952. To the north, the vast Trafalgar
tip is clothed with conifers, and surmounted by a fire observation
post.

Beyond Serridge Jcn the single line was in a cutting, with the
Trafalgar tip an ever-increasing menace. In 1887 a serious slip
occurred, and a retaining wall, with a buttress over the line, was
built in 1904. The first connection to Trafalgar was a loop on the
main line with two sidings into the colliery. Beyond, on the down
side, a gate marks the later (1890) connection to Trafalgar, a 15-
chain siding to the screens.

At Drybrook Road station (17 miles 32 chains), in a charming
setting, the west connection of the loop to the main line was a
double slip so that Trafalgar traffic could run direct to Bilson Jcn or
on to the Mineral Loop. The course falls past a connection to Crump
Meadow colliery, to Laymoor Jcn (17 miles 69 chains), worked by a
ground frame, and the site of Bilson platform (up side). Immediately
beyond, the Trafalgar Tramway crossed on the level *en route* to
Bilson Yard, the s & w curving to its triangular junction with the
GWR Churchway branch. The tramway crossing was closed in 1890,
and in 1900 Laymoor Jcn came into being, with the extension into
Cinderford.

Although often referred to collectively as 'Bilson Jcn', the connections formed part of the GWR Bilson Yard sidings, and no
through running was normally practised, the GWR passing traffic in
at the North Jcn, and accepting it at the South Jcn; both points

were 18 miles 14 chains from Berkeley Road Jcn. Both curves had loops, and the north curve had a siding serving the old Cinderford passenger station, while the goods platform, on the south curve, was used for loading Crown timber occasionally until about 1938. Bilson South Jcn was beneath the bridge carrying the s & w line to Cinderford new station.

From Laymoor Jcn the single track traversed Laymoor Quag (quagmire) on an embankment, then crossed the GWR Churchway branch, Cinderford Brook, the GWR Whimsey line, and the formation of the Forest of Dean Tramroad, before reaching the former Cinderford Jcn (18 miles 30 chains) with the GWR Cinderford Loop. The remnant of the s & w line became part of the Forest of Dean branch, terminating at Cinderford station* (18 miles 60 chains), a single platform with a small goods yard. The FOD passenger service to Cinderford was withdrawn in 1958, and the line closed in 1967.

The whole of the Lydbrook line was unusually attractive for, like the Coleford branch, it was a 'mountaineering' line, climbing at 1 in 50 for most of its $4\frac{1}{2}$ miles from Lydbrook Jcn. At Serridge Jcn were two reception roads looped to the running line, beyond which the track passed through woodland on to a 180-degree curve around a hill on a radius of about 7 chains, running due north at Speculation siding; this loop was laid when Speculation colliery ceased production, to supply coal to the pumping engines, used to drain Trafalgar. The siding existed in 1877, and Crawshay & Co. lifted it in 1926. The ruins of the boiler house remain, also the once awesome stone-lined shaft, now filled in.

Mierystock siding (17 miles 38 chains), dating from 1874, consisted of a loop, with a spur to a wharf, for loading coal brought on a short surviving stretch of tramroad from Speculation colliery; in 1915 two tracks were laid, to inwards and outwards loop sidings which crossed the hillside above the tunnel to the screens of the reopened Arthur & Edward colliery. The main line, falling in cutting, passed under a bridge and then into Mierystock tunnel, 242 yd long, at the exit of which was Brierley siding, laid in 1887 to serve quarries; by 1930 it was little used and was removed in 1936.

The route crosses the tramroad twice by bridges and then runs on the hillside, with the wooded valley on the down side. On the up side stood until recently tramroad mile-post $5\frac{1}{2}$, well away from the tramroad route and not in accord with the system of tramroad mile-posts. A dilapidated stone abutment, on the up side, is a relic of Waterloo colliery (otherwise known as the Pludds), opened about 1892 by Richard Thomas & Co. The pit, high on the hillside, in 1908

* Demolished 1968.

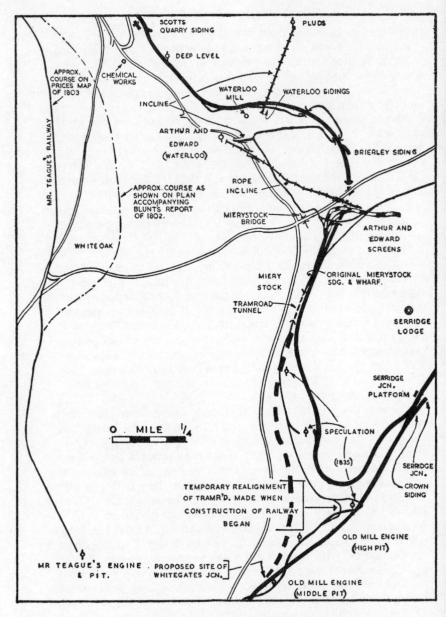

Map No. 7. Serridge Jcn and Mierystock

sent some 300 tons daily down a self-acting incline to sidings connected with the main line in one direction only, all traffic having to go to Upper Lydbrook for marshalling. The pit was closed and the sidings removed in 1916.

Far below on the down side was the Arthur & Edward pithead, its puffing, clanging winding engine now a memory. The route runs on the open hillside, passing the disused Scott's quarry, which had a short-lived siding in 1877. By the road below was Lydbrook chemical works (closed about 1919), which sent charcoal, blacking and naptha by road to Upper Lydbrook station.

Passing the church, a worthy structure of local stone consecrated in 1851, the crossing loop began just before the level crossing, and immediately beyond was Upper Lydbrook station (18 miles 78 chains). The signal box (of GWR type) was on the down platform; the original box stood on the up platform, both existing about 1912. The two sidings behind the down platform had a shunting spur, into which down trains could run direct, whilst up trains backed in; in 1908 the up connection was removed, a scissors connection was made between the down line and the spur, and a siding was added for Waterloo traffic. The line soon passed through Coles Rock tunnel (1 chain), a lofty unlined gash through a rock outcrop.

In the valley is the site of Russell's wireworks, and imagination pictures the waterwheel, the Limekiln pool, and the scrap-fed cupola with its fiery stream of iron. The valley is now quiet, and the hills, mostly wooded, form a charming background to the ever-changing view from the railway.

Hillview House, on the up side, was built by the S & W to replace its namesake, in the railway's path. On the down side the wireworks incline comes up; it was diverted when the railway was built, for transhipment at the end of a long siding from Lower Lydbrook. This passed over a weighbridge, and also served the Lydbrook tinplate-works incline (worked by S & W locomotives). The siding (shortened by 1901, due to Russell's works closing) was removed in 1938, when its two ground frames were closed.

Immediately beyond the site of Lower Lydbrook station (19 miles 63 chains, no goods facilities) was Lydbrook viaduct, giving a fine view of the Wye, and the route beyond crosses Offa's Dyke. Bicknor siding was laid in 1888 because the S & W frequently lost traffic to the GWR at Lydbrook Jcn, for want of accommodation.

The Ross & Monmouth line approached on the up side, crossing the Wye, with the Ediswan works intervening. An underbridge here (now removed) was suitable for double track, but the line did not double before the approach to the GWR Lydbrook Jcn station (20 miles 60 chains). The junction, with crossovers in both directions, was at 20 miles 69 chains, with s & w sidings beyond. s & w trains used one face of the island platform (another platform, on the s & w down side, was apparently used for loading goods). The passenger service was withdrawn from the R & M line in January 1959 and the section from Lydbrook Jcn to Monmouth (May Hill) was closed completely, followed by that to Ross, in 1965.

THE MINERAL LOOP LINE

This line, some 6½ miles long, involved much heavy work. Billups began work on 1 September 1870, and the line was opened for mineral traffic on the standard gauge from Crump Meadow colliery to Lydney harbour on 22 April 1872; the conversion of the broad gauge took place on 11-12 May, so for nearly a month the s & w presented a unique operating feature, broad, standard and tram locomotives and tram horses all in use, with mixed gauge south of Tufts Jcn. On 21 May the directors were taken up the line nearly to Trafalgar colliery; work was not quite complete there, but by mid-June the Loop was extended to join the main line at Wimberry.

Although carrying heavy traffic, the Loop was worked for many years without any form of traffic regulation. By 1894 electric bells had been installed at Tufts Jcn and Moseley Green, and up trains received 'line clear' by bell code from Tufts before leaving Moseley Green, the line to Lydney Town being kept clear in case of runaways. Trains were sorted at the pretentiously-styled 'gravitation shunting sidings' at Moseley Green (New Fancy), engines taking water at the lower end 'to be out of the way and to stop any runaway wagons'. The Loop was worked by the same engine through the day, re-fuelling at Tufts Jcn. In 1895 a man was appointed at 21s per week to regulate traffic, but this solitary guardian was unable (not surprisingly) to exercise much sway over the northern part from his hut beneath Moseley Green water tower.

The section from Drybrook Road to Foxes Bridge was normally worked independently from Drybrook Road, and in 1897 instructions were issued that no Loop train was to leave there until any preceding train, if due to return, had done so; if the train was going through to Tufts Jcn, that following was to wait ten minutes before proceeding cautiously, but it could take wagons as far as Crump Meadow, after the crew had been warned. These lax arrangements led to an accident in 1903 (see Chapter 11). Colonel Yorke, Board of Trade, criticised severely the system of working, 'if system it could be called. The line in fact, though seven miles long, has been worked with less care than a station siding, for upon the latter there are shunters and yardmen to direct the movements . . . whereas on the former there was no one.'

Later in 1903 the Loop was divided into three sections, Drybrook Road to Crump Meadow, regulated by pilot guard, Crump Meadow to Foxes Bridge, and Foxes Bridge to Tufts Jcn, both worked by train staff. The Crump Meadow staff was housed in a box on the Foxes Bridge signal post, and had to be fetched from or returned to that place on foot. Trains were frequently banked up to Moseley Green or Lightmoor, when the bank engine carried the staff, returning without it, light or with a train, to Tufts. Brick Pit siding and signal were worked by one lever, electrically controlled from Tufts Jcn, a refinement introduced in 1903—1906.

In 1922 the Drybrook Road—Crump Meadow section was equipped with a staff, kept at Drybrook Road and controlling the signal at Crump Meadow. If a train was due to enter from Crump Meadow, the signalman at Drybrook Road had to take the staff there. In July 1912 there were seven down (i.e., northbound) and six up trains, three each way running 'as required'. None ran beyond Crump Meadow, but two main-line trains worked from Drybrook Road to Foxes Bridge and back. By 1932 there was only one regular train, to Drybrook Road and back.

On 1 April 1942 the Ministry of Works requisitioned Moseley Green tunnel, the track being removed. New Fancy output, only about 50 tons weekly, was worked *via* Drybrook Road, using one train staff. Ammunition traffic for the tunnel was propelled, brake van leading, from Tufts. The track between the tunnel and Blakeney Road bridge was removed on 21 October 1942, but increased traffic at Acorn Patch depot led to the tunnel being derequisitioned as from 22 November 1943, the Loop being restored as a through line on 29 December, and worked throughout with one staff. The Blakeney bridge, which had been temporarily strengthened, was demolished with explosives on 13 March 1951, as unsafe, and the track was broken north of Pillowell siding. Several journeys were worked (the last on 16 June 1953) to clear ammunition from Acorn Patch, the route being Lydney, Bullo Pill, Cinderford exchange sidings, Laymoor Jcn and Drybrook Road, as the junctions at Serridge and Cinderford had been broken. Track lifting north of Pillowell commenced in September 1956, but daily coal traffic continued from

Pillowell until 30 November 1957, the track thence to Tufts Jcn being lifted in December.

Leaving Tufts Jcn (whence distances will be given), a siding extended to Whitecroft station, originally joining the main line there and serving the Patent Fuel works. The single track bore away into a cutting, to Pillowell Level, where the four original sidings were lifted in 1898 when the level closed. A shaft was driven, and three sidings were opened in December 1939; some coal went only 1½ miles, to the power station at Norchard.

The line crossed a small girder bridge with stone arch approaches, then a level crossing, followed by a cutting with a footbridge. Phipps's siding, serving a coal pit, was removed before 1892. For nearly a mile the track climbed steadily on an embankment in the shallow Rudge Brook valley, to the south portal (1 mile 67 chains) of the 503-yd Moseley Green tunnel, dated 1871 and preceded by a van siding and platform, both added in 1942. Beyond the tunnel was Moseley Green (or Brick Pit) siding, a loop from which a short private branch, worked by the s & w, ran to the colliery. The siding was removed in 1943.

An embankment brings the route to the Blakeney Road underbridge; beyond, there was a long loop (at one time two), a water tank on the up side, and the connection (2 miles 63 chains) to New Fancy colliery. The 22-chain branch, laid beside the broad-gauge branch from the Central line in 1872, was worked by the s & w. The pit produced prolifically, as witness its immense conical tip (later a fire observation post), being closed in August 1944.

The route is straight for half-a-mile through Middleridge Inclosure, until it crosses Blackpool Brook by a substantial bridge, built for the Central Railway (which never reached it) and hence known as 'Central Bridge' until the last trains ran. A similar bridge crossed a Forest ride, the course here being on a high embankment. At 4 miles 22 chains were Acorn Patch sidings, three roads converging to an engine release neck, established in 1943 to serve a military depot.

Lightmoor pit, owned by the Crawshays, had earlier outlets to the Bullo Pill tramroad and the FOD branch. From the s & w a long loop was provided, with connections to internal lines. Production ceased in 1940, the buildings were used for military purposes, and the siding was last worked in May 1945.

Beyond a stone overbridge carrying the Speech House road was Woorgreens siding, serving an unfortunate little pit; a tramway linking it with Lightmoor was licensed in 1855, and disused by 1869. The s & w connection was not completed until 1903, and a year

THE ENGINEER AND
THE SYMBOL

(25) *George William
Keeling*

(26) *The company seal,
a fine microcosm of the
Forest scene*

HEADQUARTERS

(27) *Severn House, Lydney; Keeling's house next door and, beyond, the cottage occupied by his coachman, Saunders*

(28) *Lydney locomotive sheds in July 1939*

later the pit was closed. It was later re-opened, but closed finally in 1912, a length of line on s & w land remaining until 1938.

A loop served Foxes Bridge colliery by two connections at the north end, and a rope-worked incline went to the FOD branch. A second connection, of about 1895, to the north, was used for outward traffic, the original carrying inwards empties, until production ceased in 1931. At the northernmost Loop line colliery, Crump Meadow, the original connection (6 miles 21 chains) was later extended to a further trailing junction. Coal continued to go out on the GWR, because every loaded truck had to be hauled up a long incline to the s & w by four horses, but in 1882 a half-mile private line was constructed to the s & w near Laymoor, enabling trucks to be moved entirely by gravity, empties coming in from the Loop while loaded wagons went to Laymoor and to the GWR. The pit was closed in 1929. A loop siding preceded the junction at Drybrook Road (6 miles 49 chains), which was virtually equidistant from Berkeley Road Jcn by both the main line and Loop line (17 miles 29 chains by the latter).

The OAKWOOD branch, 71 chains long, began as a broad-gauge siding laid to Tufts loading bank, and was extended along the tramroad as needed, to Parkhill Level (1874) and to Dyke's (or Whitecroft) Level, Captain Ross lending the s & w £500 for this purpose in 1876. The authorised extension was fenced as far as the proposed 'Knockley Gate Jcn', and in 1890—1891 the track was taken on to Parkgutter pit, but no further.

Traffic was always controlled by train staff, the vehicles being propelled up from Parkhill Loop to Princess Royal. At Tufts Jcn, the loading bank is on the down side, the centre of three tracks was the running road. The high bank has two levels; a tramway from South Oakwood iron level used the upper level, with a tip and chute, while a tramway from Tufts iron level came round on the terrace; both lines were disused by 1920, but a small wood distillation works near the bank was open until 1946, giving some cordwood and outgoing charcoal traffic. On the up side was Morgan's chemical works siding, lifted in 1906.

Parkhill sidings, a loop with three tracks to a wharf on which a tramway from the level terminated, handled ironstone from Crawshay's mine, and coal also in the early 1900s. The connection was removed in 1919, replaced later, and lifted in 1935 on the closing of Parkhill colliery.

Whitecroft level loading bank, on the up side, had a siding, and a brickworks on the down side preceded Parkgutter (Princess Royal) colliery, completed in 1915. The branch terminated in empty wagon sidings in the Forest. A private rope-worked tramway was laid from Flour Mill colliery (opened 1874—1875, closed 1931), down to a loading dock at Parkgutter. Princess Royal closed as a mine in March 1962, but continued in use for pumping, screening and rail-loading the coal being worked from the re-opened Pillowell shaft, this requiring two or three trains weekly, instead of the daily work-ing. Closure of the branch is noted in Appendix 1.

THE COLEFORD BRANCH

The s & w had to build its Coleford line without delay, for other-wise the Coleford Railway could have extended as far south as Gorse Hill. The contractors were Robinson & Adams of Bristol. Difficulty was experienced from quarry owners claiming land re-quired, but in January 1874 the committee noted with satisfaction that the time for the Coleford Railway to build its extension would expire on 1 August. The branch was opened for mineral traffic on 19 July 1875, and iron ore from the Crown estate of High Meadow was soon being carried. The branch was formally opened for pas-senger traffic on Thursday 9 December 1875 and Coleford, the Forest 'capital', having waited 22 years for its railway (the CMU & PR Act was passed in 1853), did full justice to the occasion.

In the market place young fir trees were placed, evergreen arches spanned the streets, posters proclaimed 'Long looked for, come at last' and 'Success to the 7 and Y'. A general holiday was kept, and at one o'clock a cheering crowd greeted the first train, the engine decked with flowers and holly. 'Welcome to Coleford, gentlemen', said Sir James Campbell, the Crown Surveyor, shaking hands with Graham Clarke, the chairman.

At a luncheon in the Town Hall, Campbell said that larger and richer companies had talked of making the line, but their old and tried friends the s & w had quietly stepped in and done it; perhaps they had felt their way a little too much, but it had all come right at last. Clarke said that they did not sound the trumpet before, but set to work like one of the Forest collieries—Strip And At It. They had been called an antediluvian railway, told that conversion was impossible, and that some great scheme would swallow them up. (Laughter.) But they had not been swallowed up yet. (Cheers.) At night the streets were crowded with visitors from the villages, en-joying the festivities, the public ball and the illuminations, which included a gas-lit locomotive picture in front of the Town Hall. The regular passenger and mail service commenced on the following morning.

In January 1876 two passenger trains ran each way between Lydney and Coleford, plus connections (one down, two up) to main-line trains, but in 1879 there was only one through train each way, plus the connections. In later years the train generally consisted of two carriages picked up from the main-line train at Coleford Jcn, tickets having been examined at Parkend.

Like its predecessor, the Milkwall branch, the line curved almost continuously, and climbed for most of its 3¾ miles at about 1 in 30. Traffic was always controlled by train staff, and the regulations of 1894 limited up trains (i.e. towards Coleford Jcn) to eight loaded wagons, to be braked and pulled down. Futterhill siding was normally worked by a separate journey, speed being limited to 15 m.p.h. for up passenger trains, and 10 m.p.h. for up goods. In July 1912 there were five down and six up passenger and three goods trains, one goods running only if required.

Leaving Coleford Jcn the single line began to climb, and curved above a sawmill on the down side; the Forest closed in, the gradient stiffened, and the sight and sound of a pair of pannier-tank engines ascending the bank was memorable. The line turned through nearly a half-circle, passing the site of Venus (later Great Western) colliery, the siding of which was removed before 1917.

The road is below, in the trees of Quest Slade, on the up side Bostonbury Hill rises sharply, and the line curved to cross the tram-road tunnel. At 1 mile 35 chains from Coleford Jcn was Point Quarry (Darkhill) siding, and for the next half-mile there is a maze of old coal shafts, quarries and ruined works. On the down side the lengthy Futterhill siding (sometimes dignified as a 'branch') had two connections, and terminated in two sidings by the roadside, opposite Darkhill firebrick works, now a ruin; intermediately there was a loop and siding for Darkhill level, and later a short extension served a stone works, with a loop and loading dock. Darkhill East ground frame was closed in 1953; Middle and West ground frames in 1957.

The little George Inn (down side) is one of the few signs of life. The line crossed the Coleford road by an iron bridge, and curved on a low embankment past the Titanic steelworks, a gaunt roofless stone ruin* latterly housing nothing more than a chicken run. In a shallow cutting are the abutments of the bridge which carried the tramroad temporarily, so low that it must have been of movable type. The scene is open and desolate, the ground torn by

* Demolished 1964.

past industries. Milkwall (2 miles 56 chains) had a loop siding, and the short platform had a brick building dated 1924, its wooden predecessor having been burnt; it is on the up side, with the remains of a wharf which long ago served a tramway to Gosty Knoll quarries. The station was closed entirely from 1 May 1944, and the wharf siding was removed in 1955.

A mile through fields precedes Coleford station (3 miles 58 chains), a single platform originally having a wooden office, to which a waiting room was added in 1878. The premises were destroyed by fire on 19 July 1918, and replaced in brick. Closure of the branch is noted in Appendix 1.

THE TWO COLEFORD STATIONS

On 1 September 1883 the GWR (Coleford Railway) opened its branch from Wyesham Jcn, near Monmouth, to Coleford. The S & W complained that there had been no consultation to ensure train connections, and soon the GWR practically cancelled the rates between Coleford and its stations *via* the S & W, without notice.

The GWR station was only a few yards from the S & W's, but it was not until May 1884 that the GWR agreed to a temporary junction between the sidings 'without prejudice to an efficient junction hereafter' as the S & W put it. Four reversals would have been necessary before a S & W train could get into the GWR station, effectively preventing through working. Even this awkward connection remained unused until the S & W, after complaining of a block to traffic, instructed staff to use it on 7 December 1885.

The GWR line from Wyesham Jcn to Whitecliffe, about ¾-mile west of Coleford, was lifted in 1917, and thereafter the Coleford section could only be reached over the S & W, a sad fate for the would-be Oakwood valley invader. The 'temporary' junction remained in use for 65 years, until traffic from Whitecliffe quarries justified a direct connection, opened on 26 October 1951.

The 52-chain SLING branch left the Coleford branch opposite Milkwall platform, and a loop siding served an ochre works. The country is uninviting, the track unfenced, and the only feature was Sand siding, serving a small wharf at one time used for loading iron ore. The branch terminated at a wharf which was a railhead for tramroads serving New Ham and Sling iron pits and the British coalpit, but in 1924 F. Watkins's engineering works was established, and the branch latterly terminated at the works gate, with sidings beyond.

The PARKEND ROYAL branch, ultimately 42 chains long, was

probably laid on the broad gauge from Coleford Jcn to the road at Travellers Rest, south of which it was owned by Crawshay & Co. and known as the 'Furnace Branch', 26 chains long; it terminated in coke-yard sidings which led over the covered way to Parkend furnaces. Brookhall Ditches siding was laid in 1873, traffic from it going to the coke-yard, and in 1887 the s & w began to work up to the re-opened Parkend Royal colliery, paying Crawshay a wayleave. In 1891 the Furnace branch was sold to the colliery concern, but the s & w kept it in repair, and the joint committee assumed ownership in 1896. Traffic ceased in 1928, but the track south of Travellers Rest was not lifted until 1940. The branch was worked as a siding, empty wagons being pushed up.

CHAPTER 8

The Severn Bridge Railway

FORMATION OF THE COMPANY

The inland thrust of the Severn estuary was irksome to the traveller from South Wales, and from 1810 onwards many schemes were put forward for tunnels, bridges and ferries; but only one bore fruit, the Bristol & South Wales Union Railway, with a ferry at New Passage, being completed in 1863. Lack of money, and opposition (mainly on the grounds of impeding navigation), brought the others to naught.[1]

By 1870 a Severn bridge was urgently needed—the Gloucester & Berkeley canal was too small; bigger ships were accommodated in primitive docks at Sharpness, but often had to leave in ballast, for Sharpness had no railway to provide bunker or ballast coal or exchange freight, and Gloucester faced a serious loss of trade.

W. B. Clegram, engineer of the Gloucester & Berkeley Canal Co., commissioned G. W. Keeling to survey the river and to investigate the possibilities of a bridge near Sharpness in 1865; Keeling found that the deep-water channel was constant and other factors favourable, and George Wells Owen of Westminster (who had been engineer for some minor Forest railways) joined him in furthering the scheme; plans were deposited in 1870, but it failed for want of financial support.

The year 1871 produced no fewer than six schemes; two were quickly withdrawn, a third, the Severn Tunnel Railway, securing its Act in 1872. The others all had the same title—the Severn Bridge Railway—and were numbered for Parliamentary purposes.

No. 1. From the South Wales line east of Chepstow bridge to the B & SWUR, with a viaduct at Aust Cliff, and a branch to Thornbury. This bill failed to comply with standing orders.

No. 2. A railway and roadway viaduct at Sharpness.

No. 3. From the SWR line west of Portskewett, over the Shoots by a viaduct, to the B & SWUR near New Passage station. This bill was abandoned.

Railway No. 2 was energetically backed by the G & B Canal Co. (then constructing large docks at Sharpness), the S & W and others. The Midland Railway and the G & BC guaranteed 4½ per cent on a £75,000 debenture loan. Opponents included the GWR (interference with shipping at Bullo Pill) and a conservative S & W faction, while the MR petitioned 'to keep the line free for all railway companies'.

The Severn Bridge Railway Act of 18 July 1872[2] authorised a railway 4 miles 1 furlong in length from Lydney (SWR line) to Holly Hazle (Sharpness), with short branches to the S & W near Lydney Church and into Sharpness docks, also a footroad toll-bridge (not made). The authorised capital was £225,000, and to offset the high cost the company was to regard the bridge as 3 miles long for charging purposes. The GWR, MR, S & W and G & BC Companies were all authorised by this and subsequent Acts to subscribe heavily, and all did so except the GWR. The chairman was William Charles Lucy (chairman of the G & B Canal Co.) and the directors included MR representatives, W. B. Clegram, H. R. Lückes and Edwin Crawshay. By its Act of 25 July 1872 the MR was authorised to build a branch some 4 miles long from Berkeley Road to the docks at Sharpness, this being opened for goods traffic on 2 August 1875, and for passengers on 1 August 1876.

THE S & W BETWEEN TWO FIRES

After the South Wales settlement of £15,000, the GWR and S & W rarely came into contact without protracted discussions, the GWR high-handed, obstructive, cavilling at the most reasonable request, the S & W exhibiting deference and conciliation—considerable diplomacy was called for from its officers. The Forest company always fiercely opposed any threatened invasion of its territory, but had confined itself to the Forest, carrying to the nearest river or railway. In supporting the Severn Bridge scheme it was venturing further afield, into contact with another great company, and moreover one for which the GWR had little love, the Midland.

In March 1872 the SBR Co. asked if the S & W would work its line, and suggested an early application for running powers to Stroud and Nailsworth if required, for inclusion in the current Midland bill. The S & W pledged support, but added that a contribution would be unlikely, in view of its own programme. G. W. Keeling had explained to the S & W board in January that he had kept in view its interests, had avoided associating the bridge with a large railway scheme (which might have failed completely, as others had done), and had laid it out 'to offer the best compromise for settling a vexed question between the GWR and Midland companies'. The capital required was so large that both were asked to subscribe, and on 22 November 1873 the Keelings met James Allport, general manager of the MR, at Derby.

Allport wanted running powers over the S & W, which he said would probably not be used, offering in return powers to Bristol and Stroud. The Keelings explained that the GWR might injure their company if they made an agreement with the MR. Allport replied that the GWR could not injure the S & W without injuring the MR, 'who would have the means of retaliating'. G. W. Keeling met Allport again, at Sharpness, but there were signs that the MR might prove as difficult a neighbour as the GWR, and G. B. Keeling wrote, 'our impressions of the understanding . . . somewhat differ'. A draft agreement of February 1874 gave the MR running powers over the whole S & W system, fixing its own rates and fares—the S & W was to add the running powers it required. This 'blank cheque' was of little value, for the S & W was unlikely to have the equipment to go far beyond the Forest, even if it so wanted.

The S & W board was torn by grave doubts. Would the agreement prevent it selling its line to the GWR in the future—or, indeed, to the MR? If so, would it not be better to force a purchase on Derby instead? Or again, if it declined, would the bridge be lost—and would it be better to lose the bridge than to be bound to the MR? Mr Coates, the S & W Parliamentary agent, did not believe that the company could remain independent without perpetual conflict with its powerful neighbours. The more valuable its traffic became, the more keenly would the GWR scheme to get it—'already they hem you in on all sides'. Coates added that recent legislation promised to make the company part of a great through line, and the MR was the most likely purchaser—the GWR might bid to thwart the MR, but not from any conviction of usefulness to itself. He advised rejection of the agreement, even if the bridge depended on it, unless the MR ensured a minimum traffic or income, and the invitation of an MR offer of purchase.

The S & W declined the agreement, and saved its soul, but only temporarily. Lucy regretted the decision, and urged reconsideration, probably realising that the MR could make or break his company. Nevertheless in July 1874 it was reported that the MR had decided to subscribe £50,000, and all appeared well. Little was heard from the GWR, but in its Act of 1877, permission was given for the S & W to enter into agreements for the working, maintenance and use by the GWR of the S & W railways and works. The SBR Co. decided to make the swing bridge, tunnel and earthworks suitable for double track, and an Act of 2 August 1877 authorised the raising of an additional £133,300 and an extension of time until July 1880.[3]

In 1878 the bridge was taking shape, and more money was needed. The S & W board was disconcerted to learn in March that the MR declined to take up its preference shares unless given running powers over the S & W—a cunningly-timed bombshell. A joint meeting of the S & W and SB companies was hastily called, at which Lucy suggested an amalgamation. Agreement was soon reached, granting the MR running powers over the whole of the S & W, reciprocal powers to the S & W from Sharpness to Nailsworth and Stroud, and full facilities for S & W traffic to Bristol, Bath, Gloucester and over the Somerset & Dorset line. The bridge was saved, but S & W territory was no longer inviolate. MR presence was not greatly felt, but it had obtained the essential foothold and the line might otherwise well have fallen to the GWR alone in 1894.

BUILDING THE BRIDGE

Early in 1875 contracts were let for the bridge, to Hamilton's Windsor Iron Co. of Garston, at £190,000, and for the railway approaches, to Vickers & Cooke of London, at £90,000. The bridge was a series of bowstring girders resting on piers of cylindrical columns. The northern approach was over 13 arches of Forest stone. The bridge, with approach, was 4,162 ft long, the river was 3,558 ft wide at the crossing, and 30 miles were saved on a Chepstow—Bristol journey.

The two spans over the main channel were 327 ft long and 39 ft deep. The pier diameter was 10 ft below low-water level and 7 ft above, the headway being 70 ft above high-water level. There were 19 lesser spans, and a swingbridge, and in all some 3,600 tons of cast iron and 3,500 tons of wrought iron were used. The cylinders were of cast iron, $1\frac{1}{4}$ in. to $1\frac{1}{2}$ in. thick, in 4-ft lengths. The three large piers had four columns each, the others two columns. The depth of sand at the first 12 piers averaged about 28 ft, and after No. 12 compressed air was used, a wrought iron bell being bolted to the top of the cylinder, with an air lock. The deepest piers were carried 4 ft into bedrock and Nos. 15 to 20 gave considerable difficulty, being exposed to a 10-knot tide rising 30 ft in $2\frac{1}{4}$ hours, with a depth from bedrock to high-water level of 70 ft.

Staging was erected with guides to locate the cylinder sections, which were lowered by screws and chains, bolted through inside flanges, felt-lined for expansion and filled with concrete. Owing to the currents and tide rise, the spans could not be erected on shore and floated into position (as at Saltash and elsewhere), but had to be erected *in situ* over massive timber stagings. In 1876 some of the partly-erected cylinders were washed down; the two main piers lay in the river, and divers had to separate all the cylinder joints before they could be salvaged.

The swing span was 197 ft long, suitable for double track, on a central masonry pier; it weighed some 400 tons, and was turned on a ring of conical rollers by one of a pair of steam engines housed above the track. To align and lock the bridge an iron bar entered a socket on the pier, and this was used to sever telegraphic communication, so that a train could not be accepted unless the bridge was locked. Later, electric locking prevented withdrawal of a token at Severn Bridge or Sharpness boxes if the bridge was open.

Vickers & Cooke failed to prepare the way for the Iron Company, and soon Griffith Griffiths of Yorkley took over the Sharpness approaches. In September 1876 the viaduct was not commenced, only a heading for the tunnel was ready, and Vickers & Cooke were required to obtain within a month adequate labour and plant, including 200 excavators and a locomotive. Later it appeared that they had secretly transferred the contract to John Brown of Bray, Berkshire; Brown's agents visited the site in June 1877, after which Bruff, who had been 'managing' affairs there, retired, and by February 1878 Brown was asking to be released from his contract. The SBR needed no second invitation, took over the plant and gave the job to Griffiths to complete. In February 1879 the directors reported with obvious relief that the completion of the first 327-ft span 'has removed all doubt as to the construction of the second'; the deflection under its own weight, estimated at about 3 in., was only $\frac{7}{8}$ in.

High tides delayed erection of the second large span by carrying away the scaffolding, but the novel use of electric light enabled a night shift to work on staging and attend the divers, and saved eight months, because this work could only be done during neap tides, about one week in each month.

OPENING OF THE SEVERN BRIDGE

The bridge was inspected by Colonel Rich on 3 and 4 October 1879, eight locomotives and a saloon carriage first standing on each

Great Western & Midland Railway Companies Joint.

Severn and Wye and Severn Bridge Railway.

K. 7396.   *Divisional Engineer's Office,*

Gloucester,   July 4th   1904.

Dear Sir,

Severn Bridge.

   I am asked to report on the present condition of the Severn
Bridge & particularly as to the condition of the columns.
You will remember in 1900 you carried out an examination of the
columns by my instructions. Your report to me is dated May 31/1900
& no doubt you have a copy of it.
You will understand that I want the Bridge carefully examined
throughout, girders & columns, & to be furnished with particulars of
anything that you may discover.
With regard to the columns you will remember that Piers 16,17,18,19,
& 20 are the only Piers at which the ground does not ebb up at low
Tide & therefore it will be necessary for you to employ a Diver at
these Piers.   You will as before get specimens of the incrustation
& also endeavour if possible to drill holes through the cast iron
in order to ascertain the exact thickness of sound iron.

                              Yours truly,

Mr T. Scholes.

A Letter from G. W. Keeling

span, then being run over it at varying speeds, the deflection being 1½ in. for the 327-ft spans. The railway was formally opened on 17 October, when the first train, having crossed the bridge, was played out of Lydney Jcn with no less than six people on the footplate, Earl Bathurst, the Earl of Ducie (Lord Lieutenant), Lucy, Allport, W. P. Price and G. W. Keeling. The returning train exploded a fog signal at each of the 21 spans, and Lucy drove the last rivet in the centre of the bridge. The MR and GWR ran excursions from Gloucester, and a train of 23 first-class carriages conveyed the hundreds of guests, including Sir Daniel Gooch (chairman, GWR) and the vice-consuls of the German Empire, America, the Netherlands and France, to a banquet in grounds near Sharpness docks.

Lucy made passing reference to the Severn Tunnel; Sir Daniel was confident, but if Neptune should resent the iron horse, and rend the limestone rock, they would be glad to offer the GWR a high and dry way. After proposing the toast of the subscribing companies, Lucy proposed 'the health of a non-subscribing company'—the GWR. The railway had not been undertaken in a spirit of hostility to any other and they would welcome any traffic from Sir Daniel; he hoped that when he had made his tunnel he would invite them all. Gooch replied that the GWR had desired and agreed to give aid, but circumstances had prevented it. He hoped that they would be able to make traffic arrangements to mutual advantage—nothing would be wanting on his part. He offered to take them through the tunnel, but advised them to bring their umbrellas—ironically, unknown to Gooch or Lucy, the tunnel had been flooded on the previous day. Edward Jones, of the Coal Association of South Wales, made a bitter reference to the competition between Welsh and Forest coal; he looked to the tunnel to provide the Welsh outlet, and hoped that the bridge would take Forest coal into non-competitive districts.

After the Tay Bridge disaster of December 1879 some sidelong glances were directed at the Severn bridge; some of the columns had cracked, and had to be hooped. On several occasions the bridge was threatened by drifting wrecks, but ironically it was in the radar age that it was laid low, an oil barge fetching down two of the smaller spans in fog on the night of 25 October 1960. Demolition of the remaining spans is noted in Appendix 1.

THE S & W & SEVERN BRIDGE RAILWAY COMPANY

The S & W and SBR Companies were amalgamated from the opening of the bridge by Act of 21 July 1879[4], the capital accounts being kept separate and the directors remaining either in the 'Wye section' or the 'Bridge section' until 1885. The combined authorised capital was £658,280, and loan powers covered another £268,373. The bill was opposed by the GWR, and the MR petitioned but did not brief counsel. Henry Tennant, general manager of the North Eastern Railway, an amalgamation of some 33 companies, was a witness for the principle of amalgamation; GWR counsel asked him, with a touch of cynicism, 'I believe if there is anyone who ought to be a witness for amalgamation, it is yourself?' to which Tennant replied 'Yes—unless it be my friend, the general manager of the GW Company; one or other of us would be the best, I think'.

In November 1879 *Bradshaw* combined the S & W & SB timetable with that of the MR Sharpness branch, although this remained MR property until transferred to the S & W Joint line in 1894, in consideration of which the GWR paid the MR £62,475. *Bradshaw* gave connecting services to Newport, and from Gloucester and Bristol to Monmouth, over the S & W line, listing seven down trains from Berkeley Road, terminating at Lydbrook Jcn (two), Lydney Jcn (four), and Cinderford, with three Coleford and two Monmouth connections. The seven up trains to Berkeley Road started from Coleford, Lydney Jcn (three), Lydbrook Jcn (two), and Cinderford, with two Coleford and one Monmouth connections. Through trains generally waited 15 minutes or more at Lydney Jcn, where a new through station replaced the S & W platform, while at Sharpness a new joint station was provided with the MR.

On Sunday 22 May 1881 fire largely destroyed Portskewett Pier, a terminal of the Severn ferry link in the GWR Bristol to South Wales passenger service. The GWR was readily granted permission to run four trains each way *via* the Severn bridge, the first continuous passenger service between Bristol and South Wales. In the S & W directors' words 'the public were temporarily spared the inconvenience of the ferry, while performing the journey in about the same time'; it was hoped that this would become permanent, but the GWR would not thus violate the ferry steamer contract and the service, commenced on 25 May, was withdrawn on 15 June when the ferry was restored. GWR engines worked through, and a reversal was necessary at Berkeley Road.

Commencing on 7 January 1923 the diversion of the Bristol to South Wales trains on winter Sundays over the Severn bridge became a regular feature, when the engineering department had possession of the Severn tunnel, and latterly similar diversions facilitated work on the S. Wales line east of Lydney.

THE RAILWAY DESCRIBED

The s & w diverges from the former MR Gloucester to Bristol line at Berkeley Road Jcn, s & w trains using the two branch platforms. The single track curves away to Berkeley Loop Jcn (1 mile 26 chains from Berkeley Road Jcn, from which point distances will be given), where it joined the double-track GWR Berkeley Loop, nearly 1½ miles long, opened for goods traffic in 1908, and closed in 1963.

Berkeley station (2 miles 24 chains), preceded by a goods yard, has the MR characteristics of its neighbours, solidly constructed in contrast to the wooden structures of the s & w stations. At Sharpness South Jcn, formerly Oldminster Jcn (3 miles 43 chains), the goods lines diverge east of the main line and the dock lines diverge west, passing a locomotive turntable. The s & w put in a wharf and two sidings at Sharpness South in 1887, for local goods traffic. Sharpness station (4 miles 15 chains) had two platforms, with the signal box on the down platform, behind the shelter. In 1956 the down track was lifted, the box was closed and removed, a loop was provided at Sharpness South and the goods lines were severed at the station end. Sharpness station was demolished c 1967.

North of Sharpness station the line became single before passing out onto the Severn bridge, while the 57-chain s & w North Dock branch diverged to the coal tip. Each night, when rail traffic ceased, the swing bridge was opened until morning; it was swung 51 times in 1953 during daytime. The viaduct over the South Wales line preceded Severn Bridge station (5 miles 40 chains), with a passing loop, two timber platforms with wooden shelters, an MR signal box dating from 1911 on the up side, and a short siding (removed in 1956) with a cattle pen, all perched on a formidable embankment. This little-used station was closed to freight traffic from 4 March 1957. Nearby is Purton Manor farm, where Sir Walter Raleigh reputedly stayed, and which the Severn bridge engineers made their office.

Severn Bridge tunnel, 506 yd long, was of double-track width, as was the whole of the SBR except the bridge. The line curved towards the GWR at Otters Pool Jcn (7 miles 71 chains), a double-track facing connection was made with the GWR, and the s & w curved sharply into Lydney Jcn station (8 miles 15 chains), two platforms with shelters and a long footbridge to the GWR up platform across the double track West Loop (mineral lines). Beyond this point the line is described in Chapter 7.

LOCOMOTIVE RESTRICTIONS

Regulations as to the maximum axle loading on the bridge came from Derby after 1894. The largest GWR locomotives authorised were the 'Dean' 0—6—0s and the '2021' 0—6—0Ts, the former weighing some 37 tons (engine only) and the latter 38 tons, in working order. When MR ballast trains worked through to Lydney or beyond, only light Johnson 0—6—0s were used. After 1923 some small LNWR locomotives were authorised but there is no record of their use. These restrictions remained until nationalisation, but not unresisted. In 1922 the GWR was using 0—6—0s numbers 2365—74—75 on the Taunton coal trains; they differed from the 'Deans', having double frames and larger cylinders, weighing a mere 2½ tons more. This was detected by an unknown sleuth, and they were sent away from Lydney in September, being replaced by Nos. 2324, 2412 and 2574.

In 1939 the use of the bridge as a regular alternative to the Severn tunnel was considered, and the GWR suggested trying the '42XX' 2—8—0Ts (82 tons) and the '72XX' 2—8—2Ts (92½ tons). The LMSR would have none of it, war or no war, and talked of 'extensive alterations and great expenses'. Later the 43-ton Collett 0—6—0s were proposed, as they gave more protection to the engine men than the almost cabless 'Deans', but these too were refused. GWR employees at Lydney delighted to recall the inter-war occasion when a 56-ton 2—6—0 of the 'Aberdare' class was inadvertently allowed to cross with a diverted freight train. No locomotives were allowed to cross coupled together and there was a quaintly-worded ruling that no train was to cross the iron section of the bridge in less than three minutes.

After nationalisation the Western Region assumed responsibility for the bridge, and soon dispensed with Derby restrictions. As from October 1950 the '43XX' 2—6—0s (62 tons) were allowed to work the Sunday diversions, and later the Collett 0—6—0s and others were authorised. On the Sundays of 15 and 22 August 1956 tests were carried out with 'Castle' class locomotives Nos. 5018, 5042 and a train of ballast wagons. This was the severest testing that the bridge had undergone, the engines and tenders weighing nearly 250 tons; as a result strengthening was authorised, to permit the use of such engines, but was overtaken by the bridge disaster.

CHAPTER 9

The Long Decline (1879-1962)

FOREST INDUSTRY AND THE RAILWAYS

The company had modernised its system, and broken out from the confines of the Forest, but it was still subject to the fluctuating fortunes of local industry. Had the tramroads been superseded earlier, the district might have been in a better competitive position, but in the long term the natural advantages of others must have prevailed. The decline in the iron trade in the 1870s was not compensated by any expansion of the coal industry, such as took place elsewhere; output remained at about the 1870 figure of 835,000 tons, with frequent strikes and depressions which affected the s & w sorely.

During the first war, several pits were closed, and this process continued after it; in 1927 the tonnage conveyed over the 41 route miles was only 944,500 (mostly coal). Yet so limited was the accommodation that in 1929 it was said that Lydney Jcn sidings were only adequate when the coal trade was depressed, and even the GWR refuge siding was often full of empty wagons, delaying South Wales trains. Operating costs were always high, due to difficult colliery layouts and severe gradients, and the short s & w haul gave it only a small proportion of receipts.

THE LAST YEARS OF INDEPENDENCE

Sharpness docks had a great advantage over Lydney, with at least 6 ft greater depth of water, so that coasting vessels loading Forest coal could use them at both spring and neap tides, and large steamers could refuel and load coal as ballast; but the s & w staith, first used on 8 January 1880, was in the shallow canal, and a deep-water tip in the dock was not completed by the dock company until 1886. Not surprisingly, the GWR showed little enthusiasm for the Severn bridge; in 1882 shipments at Sharpness were 'still much checked by the through rates at present in force', and the Brecon & Merthyr

THE 2021s ON THE LINE

(29) No. 2080, bound for Serridge Jcn, whistles for the crossing at
Upper Lydbrook station, 1947

(30) No. 2043 at Serridge Jcn, 1948

(31) No. 2044 at Bicslade Wharf, 1948

TERMINUS AND JUNCTION

(32) *Cinderford station in 1948, with Forest of Dean branch train*
(33) *Lydbrook Jcn in 1948.* S & W *line on the right*
(34) *Lydbrook Jcn in 1948, looking south to the* S & W *sidings*

Railway urged the MR and the GWR to agree to rates and 'withdraw the block they are imposing'.

In 1882 bills were introduced for the South Wales & Severn Bridge Railway, from Lydney to Monmouth and Talybont, and for the Thames & Severn Railway, from Stroud (to which place the S & W had running powers) to Siddington, near Cirencester, over the old Thames & Severn Canal route; these would have nullified the unfavourable through rates from South Wales, and placed the S & W on a short route to London and Southampton, but both bills failed. In 1883 the rates for coal from South Wales to Sharpness *via* the bridge were reduced by 6d per ton, and arrangements were made for the conveyance of steam coal from Aberdare to Southampton *via* the bridge, commencing on 1 December; the GWR wished to run over the bridge with its own engines, for economy, but the MR objected to this at first.

Owing to prolonged Dean colliers' strikes, the directors were unable to renew or replace the debentures falling due. E. Viner Ellis of Gloucester obtained a judgment, and under a High Court order the directors were appointed managers, and the general manager and secretary, joint receivers, declaring all receipts to the Court of Chancery, which ordered distribution. In 1884, through rates from S & W stations to Bristol, Exeter and other stations *via* the Severn bridge were agreed, operative on 1 April, and later in the year the GWR began sending coal to Plymouth as well as Southampton over the bridge.

A scheme of arrangement with the creditors, and for defining shareholders' rights, was enrolled on 21 July 1885, by which the two sections of the company were completely fused, all debentures were converted to 4 per cent stock, and the receivership was ended.

In 1886 the continued refusal of the GWR to agree to general through rates over the bridge forced the S & W to appeal to the Railway Commissioners, and Orders were soon made fixing Forest and Welsh through rates; the bridge and the Severn tunnel were opened as through coal routes to many stations in the West, but in July the S & W complained that after opening the tunnel the GWR cut rates below those in force to GWR stations *via* the bridge. Rates from Bilson to GWR stations not affected by the bridge were also cut. In October the iron manufacturers gave notice that contracts must cease owing to continued depression, partly due to German competition.

The little Golden Valley Railway, to the north, proposed in 1887 an ambitious extension from Pontrilas to Monmouth, with a branch to Lydbrook, with s & w approval. The Lydbrook section was soon dropped, without notifying the s & w, but running powers were proposed over the GWR to Lydbrook Jcn, also from Monmouth to Coleford. The s & w argued that if the GWR failed to get these powers, a competing route *via* the Severn tunnel would be created, instead of a new north—south route *via* the Severn bridge. The bill failed, as did another in 1889. In July 1893 the company was contemplating, with MR support, a short connection *via* Nailsworth with the M & SWJR at Cirencester, to give connections to the MR and the LSWR—the s & w was still trying to break out of the GWR circle.

The report of August 1893 was an unhappy one. A serious depression caused the stoppage of the principal house-coal collieries in July. Earnings were not sufficient to discharge the debenture interest, again Viner Ellis secured a judgment, and the s & w was once more in Chancery. The first steps towards selling the undertaking were taken by George White of Bristol, a large stock-holder, who told the board in October 1893 that he had unsuccessfully approached the MR about three years previously; the general manager and engineer had inspected the line, and estimated that £20,000 would have to be spent to comply with Board of Trade requirements. He had recently approached the GWR and found to his surprise that it was fully aware of his previous proposals to the MR.

Notwithstanding, the two companies agreed to a joint purchase, for neither was prepared to see the other firmly entrenched in such a potentially rich traffic district. On 27 February 1894 details were approved at a special general meeting and on the next day the death of G. B. Keeling occurred; for 47 years he had guided the fortunes and aspirations of the company.

The bill to authorise the sale was only passed after prolonged opposition from such diverse interests as the LNWR, Richard Thomas & Co., Gloucester and Newport Corporations, Sharpness New Docks and G & B Navigation, Sir James Campbell, Charles Bathurst, and the holders of s & w 'A' and 'B' preference stocks. G. W. Keeling's evidence revealed that the company was unable to afford traders the facilities necessary to develop the traffic, particularly adequate sidings and engine power, nearly £10,000 being required at once for rolling stock alone. By Act of 17 August 1894[1] the undertaking was vested in the GWR and MR jointly and equally as from 1 July 1894, and the proprietors received the final report at their 30th half-yearly meeting held at the Royal Hotel, Bristol, on 23 August. Two days later the agreed sum of £477,300 was received (£951,349 had been spent on the undertaking). Debentures totalling £328,265 were discharged, £131,831 1s 1d was distributed amongst the stockholders and the company was wound up.

THE JOINT COMMITTEE

A Joint Committee was to be set up within three months of the Act, consisting of three directors from each company, and the following provisions were made:

(1) Lydney harbour to be kept open at all times.
(2) Within four years an extension to be made to Cinderford.
(3) Full facilities to be offered for traffic from any joint station, through Coleford and over the GWR without terminal charges at Coleford.
(4) The MR to transfer its Sharpness branch to the Joint Committee.

After 1894 the old excitements of railway politics became a thing of the past, but the S & W system retained much of its individuality by virtue of the joint ownership. The Great Western & Midland Railways Joint Committee administered not only the Severn & Wye Joint Railway, but the Clifton Extension Joint Railway, the Halesowen Railway, and the Joint stations at Bristol, Churchdown, Worcester and Great Malvern. In practice, most matters were settled at the Joint Officers' quarterly meetings, only important questions being passed to the Joint Committee.

John J. Petrie was appointed S & W traffic manager on 12 August 1895, being promoted to traffic manager, Midland & Great Northern Joint Railway, in 1898. His successor, J. A. Carter, retired on 31 December 1919, and the post was abolished, the two companies thereafter supervising their respective sections from Gloucester, through the GWR divisional superintendent and the MR district controller, while a joint traffic inspector at Lydney Town supervised the arrangement of trains, extra workings and staff matters.

It was first suggested that the GWR should maintain the line, with existing staff, but it was soon agreed that the Joint Committee should do so, under GWR supervision. On 1 January 1906 the line from Berkeley Road to a point 6 chains south of Coleford Jcn, and to Pillowell, was transferred to the MR for maintenance purposes, the GWR becoming responsible for the remainder. The Cinderford extension was obligatory but it was not until February 1898 that the contract was let to Mr Braddock of Manchester, at £15,000, after alternative routes had been considered.

With the railway grouping of 1923, the owning companies had become the GWR and the LMSR, and the formation of British Railways brought yet another change in management; on 9 February 1948, commercial and operating responsibility for the line was transferred to the Western Region, signal and telecommunication responsibilities on the southern (London Midland Region) section as far south as Sharpness following on 5 April. LMR block rules and regulations continued in operation south of Sharpness South.

WITHDRAWAL OF PASSENGER SERVICES

Passenger traffic began when the iron and coal industries were active and the company served the area without opposition, yet it was never heavy, and was reduced by the industrial decline, the opening of the FOD branch to Cinderford for passengers (a more direct route to Gloucester) and the advent of road services.

As early as 1901 the Coleford Town & Trade Association's request for an improved evening service to enable villagers to visit the market was rejected, the traffic manager stating that 'existing trains on the branch are unremunerative', and when Cinderford residents asked for an afternoon service in the same year it was declined because there was no probability of sufficient passengers.

The *Dean Forest Mercury* of 14 June 1929 announced the withdrawal of passenger services north of Lydney Town from 8 July and added

> It is not anticipated that there will be any outburst of public indignation . . . the truth is that the passenger railway service has not entered very fully into the life of the Forest, and since the buses have developed their splendid cross-country . . . services the railway line has been more and more neglected. . . .

Complaints were made by the Wye Valley Development Association and the town of Coleford, but a deputation was told at Paddington on 3 July that the trains only carried from one to 11 passengers, and the last train north of Lydney Town was on Saturday evening 6 July 1929, no Sunday service ever having run. So passed the trains which had earned the line its local title of 'The Sad & Weary Railway'.

At the time of withdrawal, of three trains from Lydbrook Jcn *via* Cinderford, two ran to Berkeley Road and one to Lydney Jcn. Two trains ran from Cinderford, to Berkeley Road and Lydney Jcn respectively, and five from Lydney Town to Berkeley Road. In the down direction, of eight trains from Berkeley Road, two ran to

Lydbrook Jcn, two to Cinderford, three to Lydney Town, and one (the 2.40 p.m.) to Lydney Jcn and thence to Cardiff. One train ran from Lydney Jcn to Lydbrook Jcn, and on Saturdays late evening trains were run from Lydney to Parkend. The best journey time between Lydbrook Jcn and Lydney Jcn was 59 minutes, and between Lydbrook Jcn and Berkeley Road, 1 hour 26 minutes. Coleford had two up through trains to Lydney Jcn, plus five up connections, and five down connections.

There was a proposal in 1932 to restore the service between Lydney Town and Parkend on Saturdays, as the traffic did not appear to be catered for adequately by road. The possibility of working the remaining services more economically by diesel car was also considered, four LMSR bogie coaches and six GWR four-wheelers being then used, but it was said that there would be difficulty in strengthening services, one unit could not provide all services, and there were doubts of its capabilities on a 1 in 132 gradient. From 1 January 1934 first class was withdrawn and trains were without guards, while commencing on 30 November 1936 GWR auto-units worked the service, mostly without guards.

A proposal to introduce Saturdays-only auto trips between Cinderford and Upper Lydbrook, and between Lydney Town and Parkend, led to a successful test on the first-mentioned section with auto trailer No. 8 on 27 February 1936, but the idea was dropped because it involved freight service alterations. The remaining passenger service, from Berkeley Road to Lydney Town, was fairly well patronised until it was ended abruptly by the severance of the Severn bridge in 1960. (See Appendix 1.)

TO THE PRESENT DAY

After 1929 most of the double-track sections were singled, and the electric control apparatus was removed from several single lines, staffs being substituted as detailed in Chapter 7. Freight services continued, modestly patronised, during and after the second war; engines and brake vans continued hopefully to run along the northern sections, to Cinderford and Lydbrook Jcn, long after the traffic had ceased to justify them, and for years after their last journeys the track was left in position.

The most recent of the abandonments, recorded in Chapter 7 and Appendix 1, has left Parkend as the northern railhead. Beyond is little more than the earthworks; Lydbrook viaduct, too awkwardly placed to be 'dropped' by explosives, has been dismantled, but open-cast working near Coleford has led to renewed activity at Parkend Goods, the coal being railed there. (See Appendix 1.)

The Severn Bridge accident in late 1960 dealt a further grievous blow to the s & w system, the passenger service (six up, five down) being operable only between Berkeley Road and Sharpness. Connections were provided with existing services *via* Gloucester to Lydney Jcn, augmented by one train (the 7.0 a.m.) from Lydney Jcn to Gloucester (Central) connecting with the 7.42 a.m. Gloucester (Eastgate), serving Berkeley Road. The winter Severn tunnel Sunday diversions over the bridge were re-diverted *via* Gloucester. New services were introduced on 2 January 1961, comprising only four up and three down trains, and again using existing services *via* the two Gloucester stations to serve Lydney Jcn. This arrangement continued, with Lydney Town and Severn Bridge stations closed for passengers (and the latter for goods), and the direct line on to the bridge was severed north of Sharpness station, although the track on to the bridge could be reached indirectly over the s & w docks branch, until the bridge was finally dismantled (see Appendix 1).

CHAPTER 10

The Locomotives (1864-1894)

TRAMROAD LOCOMOTIVES

The steam locomotive made a very early, if fleeting, appearance in the Forest. William Stewart, writing in 1844[1], related how, in 1814, the Park End Coal Co. paid £3,000 p.a. for haulage to Lydney. He proposed to make and maintain a locomotive at his own expense to do this work, in return for half the cost of horse haulage. The company, he said, agreed but would not enter into a written agreement, for fear of antagonising the hauliers.

Stewart completed the locomotive at Newport, transported it to Lydney and convinced the coal company that it was practical, but under its threat haulage costs had been reduced to £2,000; Stewart was offered half this sum and, discouraged, he departed leaving the locomotive in settlement of a loan. He said that the affair was well known in Newport, Chepstow and Lydney, and promised to send a drawing of the locomotive but apparently did not do so.

In 1816 Stewart was trying to interest the Monmouthshire Canal Co. in locomotive trials.[2] Although s & w records do not mention Stewart's locomotive, it was resolved on 7 November 1815 'That the Company hereby approve of any person or trader hauling coal or other articles over the railway, by steam engine, provided the engine be within the weight allowed . . . and not interrupting the general trade'. The weight applicable to wagons was a maximum per axle of 1 ton (plus tare) and two wagons had to be used for conveying one load of over 2 tons. Thus, if Stewart's locomotive weighed about the same as Trevithick's Penydarren machine—some 5 tons—it would have needed eight wheels. The Penydarren locomotive was too heavy; the plates there were 3 ft long, and weighed 61 lb.[3] The s & w plates were also 3 ft long, but only weighed 42 lb., so Stewart's locomotive did not have much chance of success, however sound mechanically. Stewart maintained that he was in complete ignorance of George Stephenson's work at the time, but he may very well have seen Trevithick's machine in 1804.

T. E. Blackwell, consultant engineer to the s & w, wrote to Daniel Gooch on 20 February 1856:

My dear Gooch,
Some friends of mine, the owners of a tramway on which there is a good deal of traffic in coals—but whose circumstances they believe do not justify them to lay out money in converting their line with its numerous branches up steep gradients into a railway system—have determined on putting at least one locomotive on their line, and they would be willing immediately to contract accordingly for . . . one efficient locomotive by way of experiment. . . .
Will you be offended if I ask if you, 'the Gooch' (spare me for my impudence) would like to undertake to perform such a service for them?—if you will not I am sure you will be yet civil—if you will—I will write you an official letter and ask you to come and look at the 'locus in quo'.
My friends prefer good dividends perhaps to the results of science as they have obtained on some railways which if carried out on their system would knock their dividends down to one-third of their present modest amount.
Let me hear from you as soon as you can and I promise if you decide on doing the needful for them you shall at least have good paymasters and decent people to speak to.
Yours always,
T. E. Blackwell.

Blackwell wrote officially on the 25th, suggesting a visit to Lydney 'where a tram carriage will be ready to take us up . . . where the locomotive is required to work'. Gooch inspected drawings of 'Marshall's Tank Engine' (a 4—4—0T built at Swindon in 1854—the first standard-gauge engine built there)[4], probably to assess wheel loadings on narrow gauge.
During March, G. B. Keeling sent to Gooch a 9-ft tramplate, a map (marked with the daily loads hauled and the proposed limits

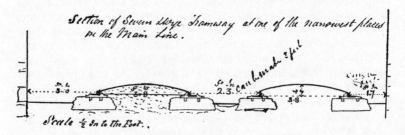

Section through the tramroad, probably at Parkend 'covered way',
from the map sent to Gooch in 1856

of locomotive working, Lydney Harbour and Wimberry Jcn) and a sketch of a typical wagon; his last letter concluded: 'I am glad to find that your report is so far favourable—and should our road not prove strong enough to bear a 12T locomotive on 4 wheels at a limited speed, we may perhaps adopt some means to strengthen it. . . .' Strangely, no reference is made in the company's minutes to this enquiry.[5]

In 1863 enquiries were once more undertaken, for by then several builders were making engines for narrow-gauge lines. In December, G. W. Keeling set out on a 'grand tour' of industrial establishments, visiting the Sheepbridge, Plymouth, Abernant, Neath Abbey, Blaenavon, Tredegar and Rhymney Ironworks.[6]

A truck weighing 1 ton net, wheels 2 in. wide on the tread, was loaded with 6 tons of tramplates and on 29 February 1864 was run between Lydney Basin and Whitecroft at various speeds from 2 to 6 m.p.h., and also up and down the Moseley Green branch, relaid with the blocks at 2-ft 6-in. instead of 3-ft pitch. The deflections of the 9-ft-long plates were greatest near the joints and when the blocks were at 3-ft pitch, and Keeling concluded that the track would be rendered suitable by shifting all the 'bearings' to 2-ft 6-in. pitch, substituting wooden sleepers at joints to maintain the gauge —even with horse haulage the blocks were constantly sinking.

On 20 April 1864, at Lydney, the directors received Keeling's report and a letter from H. H. Price of the Neath Abbey Iron Co. was read, offering to make a 3-ft 8-in.-gauge locomotive suitable for adaptation to an edge railway, for approximately £600. Cookson, the former chairman, had written from Naples expressing keen interest in this new project. Keeling summed up, 'I am sure that if the Blaenavon Tramroad will stand a 10 Ton engine rattling over it at a pace of 10 m p h several times a day—our tramway will certainly bear a 7 or 8 Ton engine at a speed of 4 or 6 m p h'. Horse power on the s & w cost approximately 1½d per ton per mile, and it was generally agreed, at the places visited, that for every six horses it was cheaper to use a locomotive.

Keeling was authorised to prepare a specification, and on 18 May 1864 tenders were considered from Neath Abbey Ironworks (£620), Alfred R. Thomas, Cardiff (£600), and Fletcher, Jennings & Co., Whitehaven (£695). Prices included delivery at Lydney and this probably accounts, in part, for Fletcher, Jennings's higher quotation. That enterprising firm, however, secured the order and the locomotive was delivered at Lydney on 31 October 1864.

No. 1 was an 0—4—0 well tank with outside cylinders 8 in. x

16 in. and cast iron wheels 2 ft 6 in. dia. (all the tramroad locomotive wheels were, of course, flangeless). The wheelbase in the makers' order book is 4 ft 6 in. but this is too small, the correct figure being nearer 6 ft 0 in. The copper firebox carried the dome with two spring-loaded safety valves. Fittings included a hand screw to wooden brake blocks on the trailing wheels, and an injector (another was added later). The locomotive was the first of the Fletcher, Jennings's patent 8-in. narrow-gauge engines.

To eliminate excessive rear overhang, the trailing (driven) axle was placed behind the firebox, and Fletcher's patent covered a special arrangement of Allan's straight-link valve gear.[7] The firebox intervening, it was not possible to fit the eccentric sheaves to the driven axle, and as outside valve gears were not in vogue the sheaves were mounted on the leading axle, and thus driven by the coupling rods. The eccentric rods led back to the expansion link, which was hung in front of the firebox, and the valve rod was set to clear the leading axle. In reversing, the link and the die block moved simultaneously and thus required less vertical space, an advantage on locomotives with small wheels and low boilers. Against this, all side-rod wear and axle-box 'knock' was transmitted to the valve gear as lost motion.

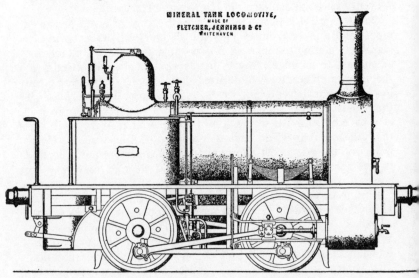

Probable form of the first S & W locomotives.
From Colburn's *Locomotive Engineering*

On 16 November 1864 G. W. Keeling reported the successful working of No. 1 and it took the directors in the company's carriage to Whitelea colliery. The Turnpike Trust soon raised the question of locomotives crossing roads, suggesting that public safety was the company's liability; if locomotives were new to the s & w, such questions were not, and the secretary replied with masterly evasion that they 'were quite willing to move with the Commissioners . . . to ensure the safety of the public without involving them in any needless expense'.

Mierystock tunnel had to be opened out to let locomotives pass onto the Churchway branch, to which a new line was laid to aid locomotive running. This branch was lightly graded, and busy; it is almost certain that locomotives did not operate on the Lydbrook section, which was little used, severely graded, and in poor shape. In December, Fletcher, Jennings offered three more 'patents' at £720 each, similar to No. 1, but having Lowmoor iron boilers instead of B.B. Staffordshire iron. Nos. 2 and 3 arrived on 14 June 1865, No. 4 on 23 August. The wheel diameter was increased to 2 ft 8 in., and a plate was fitted at the rear end instead of the rail on No. 1, but all four were without weatherboards or coke boxes.

No. 5 arrived at Lydney in November 1865, price £1,008, from Fletcher, Jennings, an 0—6—0 well tank with outside cylinders 10 in. by 20 in. and cast iron wheels 3 ft 2 in. dia. The frames were of angle-bar type and the boiler was of Lowmoor iron with a copper firebox. Fittings included two injectors, coke boxes on each side of the firebox, and hand brakes on the driving and trailing wheels. No. 5, intended for the Moseley Green branch, was the last locomotive to be numbered, and was the last tramroad locomotive. In April 1869 Keeling stated that they worked about 50,000 tons p.a. of coal down to Lydney, which over a six-day week, and at 2¼ tons per wagon (Keeling's figure), gives an average of some 70 wagon loads per day.

BROAD-GAUGE LOCOMOTIVES

The broad-gauge line did not replace the tramroad; they operated simultaneously until the system was altered to the standard gauge. When news of the belated broad-gauge venture reached Fletcher, Jennings in January 1868, they offered an 0—4—0T for £1,050, but Keeling decided to convert No. 5 at Lydney at an estimated cost of only £200. Fletcher, Jennings supplied the new wheels and axles, and in November 1868 No. 5 was ready, nearly twice as 'wide' and named *Forester;* the saddle tank was probably added at this time. Later, on standard gauge, *Forester* was the first recorded locomotive to cross the Severn bridge, on 3 September 1879.

A broad-gauge convertible locomotive from Fletcher, Jennings arrived at Lydney on 27 November 1868, named *Robin Hood,* and the first of several to bear the names of the Sherwood outlaws, the happy thought possibly originating in Highmeadow Wood, which boasted a Marian's Enclosure and, better still, a Robin Hood iron pit. The newcomer was an 0—6—0 side and back tank with outside cylinders 14 in. x 20 in. and 4 ft 0 in. dia. wheels. The boiler (of telescopic form with brass tubes), coal bunker, tanks, etc., were dimensioned to standard gauge. The axles had a third journal and wheel seat so that conversion required little more than shortening the frame stays, axles and buffer beams, and reseating one of each pair of wheels.

The middle wheels were flangeless and hand-operated wooden brake blocks to the driving and trailing wheels were fitted. It was not practicable to fit brake blocks to the leading wheels of this or subsequent outside-cylinder locomotives owing to the proximity of wheels and cylinders. In certain cases, as with *Robin Hood,* two blocks were fitted to each of the trailing wheels.

Between May and November 1869 two of the tramroad tanks, Nos. 2 and 3, were altered to broad gauge at Lydney shed, No. 2 being named *Little John.* Nos. 1 and 4 remained on the tramroad, chiefly for 'Mr Thomas's coal traffic' to Lydney basin. Keeling was advised on 25 November 1869 that he could dispose of either, but he was in no hurry to part with his hard-won locomotives—he never did 'dispose' of No. 1, as will be seen.

In 1870 the broad-gauge traffic made another convertible necessary, and the tender of the Avonside Engine Co., Bristol, at £1,880, was accepted on 4 March. They did not serve the company so well as the Whitehaven firm, delivery was delayed, and on 23 November some gear appertaining to the engine was still awaited at Lydney.

Put to stock in December 1870, *Friar Tuck* was a further 0—6—0 side and back tank with outside cylinders 16 in. x 24 in., and wheels 4 ft 3 in. dia. The boiler was domed, with flush-top firebox, all wheels were flanged, with laminated underhung springs, and brake blocks acted on the driving and trailing wheels. The slide valve gear was Stephenson's; the centre lines of the cylinders and axles coincided, and each valve rod was made in two sections with semi-circular ends which made a circle embracing the leading axle. The name was painted on the side tanks and a small front cab was fitted.

In May 1872 the GWR converted the South Wales line to the standard (4 ft 8½ in.) gauge and the S & W followed suit. By 6 January Keeling had dismantled *Friar Tuck* and sent it to Avonside for conversion, only 14 months after delivery, at a cost of £280. *Forester* and *Robin Hood* were also re-gauged in 1872 by the Bristol firm, who charged no less than £446 for *Robin Hood* and then declined to itemise the cost. Nos. 2 and 3 were also altered to standard gauge about this time, at Lydney shed. On 22 April 1872 the standard-gauge Mineral Loop line was opened and mixed gauge was used from Tufts to Lydney. By April *Friar Tuck* was running on standard gauge but the broad gauge remained up to Wimberry until May.

DISPOSAL OF THE EARLY LOCOMOTIVES

No. 4 was sold in 1872. No. 1 survived until the abolition of the tramroad and was then installed in a dredger on the canal, about 1879, as recorded by driver Ridler. It drove the buckets for many years and the boiler was repaired in 1893. Of Nos. 2 and 3, the former, *Little John*, was fitted up for inspection purposes, and was used during the busy years 1871—1875, when the works in progress needed many a hurried visit by the directors, engineer and Crown officials. One was withdrawn in 1879, the other in 1880.

The disposal of Nos. 2, 3 and 5 is an intricate story. In the first half of 1880 the S & W offered for sale two small locomotives, loaded into trucks at Lydney, £450 each, the description clearly indicating Nos. 2 and 3.[8] A sale of Hamilton's Windsor Iron Co.'s Severn Bridge plant, on 29 June 1880, at Purton and Sharpness, included three Fletcher, Jennings saddle-tank locomotives 'recently overhauled and in excellent condition'.[9] There is no record of sales to the Iron Co. in Fletcher, Jennings's list, and it is likely that the three were in fact S & W Nos. 2, 3 and 5. Nos. 2 and 3 may well have been fitted with saddle tanks on the broad or standard gauge, as was No. 5, to increase capacity and adhesive weight. They did not find buyers, for the company advertised in December 1880 two four-wheeled locomotives and one six-wheeled coupled, the dimensions indicating Nos. 2, 3 and 5.[10]

In July 1881 Keeling reported that the 'two old engines belonging to the Wye section' (Nos. 2 and 3) had been sold for £500, in November the S & W was offering two six-wheeled tanks[11], the description indicating *Forester* and *Raven* (see later), and both were offered again in late 1882.[12] *Forester* was officially withdrawn from service in 1882 and sold by May 1883 for £420.

There is no record of *Robin Hood* being rebuilt, and indeed its only record is of being twice involved in accidents. Colonel Rich concluded that its derailment on a passenger train (August 1881) was due to poor permanent way, but said, 'It cannot be a very steady engine at any time when running fast and particularly so when attached to a light train', due to its outside cylinders, very short wheelbase and short springs. On 16 March 1882 Ridler, with *Robin Hood* bunker first on the 7.34 a.m. up passenger from Lydney Town, emerged from the tunnel at Severn Bridge in dense fog and struck the brake van of a train of Welsh coal which was fouling the loop points, without derailment. Colonel Rich censured the company (the coal-train driver carried no train staff), the signalman and Ridler.

A photograph taken at Lydney Town, probably about 1890, shows *Robin Hood* somewhat modified, with the weatherboard on the bunker and Avonside cab, possibly the *Friar's* old one. Apart from the unkind things said by Colonel Rich, the small cylinders made *Robin Hood* easily 'winded' on heavy gradients and as 16-in. engines became available its star gradually set. Nevertheless it was kept spotless, latterly with bright-red side and connecting rods; by 1894 it was mainly used for banking, shunting and ballasting duties.

By April 1891 *Friar Tuck* required new cylinders and firebox, a repair beyond the capacity of Lydney shops, and it was sent to the makers. The side tanks were lengthened, the well tank removed, and the vacuum brake fitted, also probably the overall cab.

'MAID MARIAN' AND LE CHATELIER'S BRAKE

The first standard-gauge locomotives were Nos. 2, 3, *Forester*, and the two convertibles. A further 0—6—0 tank locomotive, *Maid Marian*, was ordered in January 1872, at £2,190, but Avonside again delayed delivery and it did not arrive until December, after which there was a month's work at Lydney before it could be put to traffic. Avonside did some rebuilding later, but supplied no further locomotives and even before *Maid Marian* was ready, Keeling met Fletcher in Birmingham to discuss a new locomotive.

Maid Marian's name appeared on a brass plate on the tank, henceforth a standard feature. It had outside 15 in. x 22 in. cylinders, 4 ft 0 in. dia. wheels and Stephenson link valve gear identical to *Friar Tuck's*. Other features were the slender front cab, side tanks only, a very small coal bunker, front and back sand, and hand-operated wooden brakes, but in the matter of braking *Maid Marian* differed from nearly every other locomotive in the country.

The first railways were not severely graded, but those under construction had long stretches at 1 in 40 and 1 in 50, while the Coleford branch was to rise at 1 in 30-31 for over 2 miles. Passenger trains were to be worked over most of these inclines, yet the locomotives had only hand-operated wooden blocks to driving and trailing wheels. As power brakes and cast iron blocks were still in the future, *Maid Marian* was additionally equipped with the counter-pressure braking system, introduced in France by L. le Chatelier in 1865, widely used on the Continent, and tried without success on the LNWR and the MR in 1869—1870.

From the earliest days enginemen made emergency stops by reversing and opening the regulator, but this caused gases and ashes from the smokebox to be sucked into the cylinders and pumped into the boiler. In the counter-pressure system a spray of water and steam, admitted to the hot cylinders to exclude the ashes, was turned immediately to steam and pumped into the boiler. Approaching a gradient the regulator was closed and the engine reversed, the brake cock on the footplate was then opened and the lever placed in the first notch of back gear; the regulator was re-opened and the lever notched back until the required braking was obtained, produced by the work done on the piston by the momentum of the train. At the bottom of the incline the lever was gradually moved to the first back-gear notch, the regulator closed, the brake cock shut and the cylinders emptied; the lever was put in fore gear and the regulator re-opened. Poor handling could produce serious results. Braking could be very sudden; if the spray contained too much steam the cylinder lubrication dried up, if too much water the cylinder ends could be blown off. The exhaust from the chimney was a spray of steam and water, and the driver had to keep them in correct proportion.

The only other S & W locomotive with counter-pressure brakes was *Will Scarlet*, and there can be little doubt that it was only an experiment. Chain brakes were adopted for the passenger trains, until in 1889 automatic brakes were made compulsory; goods trains always had to rely on the all-too-familiar 'pinning down' method, while in bad weather or emergency, plain engine-reversing and its evils remained the fashion.[13]

Maid Marian became the 'top-link' passenger engine, usually driven by Ridler. When the Coleford branch was opened in 1875, *Maid Marian* worked the first passenger train and in 1879 Ridler and the *Maid* worked the first ordinary train from Lydney to Sharpness. Some years later the *Maid* was involved when Richard Thomas had temporarily to close Lydbrook tin-plate works. He intended to sell some 500 boxes of tin-plate, but his employees decided that it represented their overdue wages and at night dislodged tons of rubble on to the awkward rail approach. The unsuspecting agent, loading completed, wired Lydney for an engine and anon came Ridler with *Maid Marian*, but only as far as the obstruction, whence he was obliged to return light engine to Lydney.

Maid Marian normally worked the midday passenger train to Lydbrook Jcn, then a pick-up goods to Upper Lydbrook or Serridge Jcn, clearing the Tin Works *en route*, and returning light to Lydbrook Jcn for the afternoon passenger train. She always ran bunker first into the Forest, travelling backwards down the Tin Works incline (approximately 1 in 25) so that the firebox was covered with water. Similarly, locomotives for the Coleford trains usually left Lydney bunker first, in order to be 'right way round' on the 1 in 30. There was never a turntable at Lydney, and engines were turned either by running up the mineral loop and back on the main line, or on the triangular junction at Bilson.

Maid Marian was the first s & w locomotive to have the vacuum brake (Lydney, June 1891). In June 1893 a new boiler with copper firebox, supplied by the Lowca Engine Co. (formerly Fletcher, Jennings), was fitted at Lydney. A back weatherboard was added to the bunker, and later an enclosed cab. Finally on the s & w *Maid Marian* boasted two draught-excluding sliding cab doors, seldom used, and was the only s & w locomotive to have a 'pull out' regulator handle.

The railway extensions of the 1870s further taxed the small stud; in addition to maintaining the traffic they hauled spoil and materials to the new lines, on hire to the contractors. By May 1872 they had thus earned £675 15s 0d.

The late arrival of *Maid Marian* forced Keeling to hire a locomotive from Isaac Boulton of Ashton-under-Lyne, an 0—6—0 side tank named *Hercules*, acquired in October 1872 for £500 and sent straight to Lydney. In the next two months the s & w paid £100 for the use of it, after which it was returned. *Hercules* had outside cylinders 16 in. x 24 in., wheels 4 ft 6 in. dia., no cab or weatherboard, and massive side tanks hid the boiler from view. In November an unsuccessful offer was made to the Metropolitan Railway for one of the 0—6—0 tanks built by the Worcester Engine Co., but found too heavy for the St John's Wood line.

LYDNEY HARBOUR AND CANAL

(35) *The approach over the level crossing, looking north, 1947*

(36) *Harbour entrance in 1949*

(37) *Upper Basin, 1947. Note the gabled houses of Cookson Terrace, S & W-built, to their left the old building of 1813, and remains of two tips*

THE SEVERN BRIDGE

(38) *The broken giant, 1963*

(39) *Sharpness Docks, with the Severn Bridge beyond. The* s & w *North Dock branch passes over the swing bridge; the* s & w *coal tip is on the canal beyond*

MORE LOCOMOTIVES FROM WHITEHAVEN

The outcome of the Birmingham meeting was that Fletcher, Jennings supplied the next three new locomotives, all 0—6—0 side-tank type with outside cylinders. In February 1873 the first was ordered at £2,500, to be named *Will Scarlet*, but it did not arrive until December. The cab, with curved side-sheets, was still open at the rear and the counter-pressure brake was fitted.

A new *Little John* was ordered primarily for the extension to Lydbrook Jcn, and arrived on 23 November 1874, almost identical to *Will Scarlet*. *Alan-a-Dale* was delivered in mid-1876 and owing to depressed conditions was paid for on the 'redemption principle', probably accounting for the building dates of 1878 or 1879 sometimes shown.

These three general-purpose locomotives were never fitted with vacuum brakes on the s & w and were almost exclusively used on goods trains. Their regulator handles tended to fly open, and had to be secured closed by a pin, hence probably the reluctance to use them on passenger trains. In 1893 the fireman on *Alan-a-Dale* failed to replace the pin after moving the engine outside Lydney shed and it started away unmanned, damaging the shed and *Wye*. *Will Scarlet* was used to test the Severn Bridge, crossing over coupled to *Friar Tuck* on 15 September 1879, and taking 20 loaded wagons across on 2 October. In 1894 *Little John* was rebuilt at Lydney, the Lowca Engine Co. supplying a new boiler and firebox, and new frames with cast steel axlebox guides and cylinders already fitted; appearance was little changed, except for Ramsbottom safety valves.

No further new locomotives had outside cylinders. Keeling had realised that maintenance facilities were going to be limited and had avoided cranked axles, but the necessity for a short wheelbase resulted in unsteady running, the rigid frame stay afforded by inside cylinders was lost, and it was impossible to fit leading brake blocks. The picture up to 1880 is of inadequately-braked locomotives lurching along mediocre permanent way, but they were sturdily constructed and some performed many years of arduous shunting duties after 1895.

'RANGER'—THE MYSTERY ENGINE

In 1875 the s & w acquired an 0—6—0 tender engine of LNWR origin at what appeared to be a bargain price, £800, from the

K

Northampton & Banbury Junction Railway, an impecunious little concern, closely allied to the LNWR. In 1872—1875 the NBJR reports return only two tender engines, both ex-LNWR, and one of these, No. 5, was purchased by the S & W, for NBJR accounts of 1876 show 'Balance of hire and purchase of engine No. 5 including repair, £956 18s 11d, less realised by sale of same £800'.

The basic particulars of the two 0—6—0s were:

LNW No.	Builder	Wks. No.	Date	Wheels	Cyls.	N & BJ Purchase Price
1827	Tayleur	382	1855	5' 0"	17" x 24"	£700
1849	Hawthorn	708	1848/9	5' 0"	18" x 24"	£1,000

Circumstantial evidence points to No. 1849 as being No. 5.

(1) No. 1827 was a double-framed engine weighing nearly 30 tons, not a particularly 'light locomotive', the description applied to No. 5 by Keeling.

(2) No. 1849 was an older, less robust engine of 'long-boiler' type. Swindon records note that *Ranger's* boiler was short-ened by about 2 ft 6 in. in the 1891 rebuilding, which drastic surgery suggests a long boiler originally.

(3) The price paid—£800—was more compatible with that paid by the NBJ for No. 1849 than for No. 1827.

After 'No. 5' arrived at Lydney, Keeling reported on 11 November 1875 that it was not available for service, and he proposed to modify it. As a tender engine, with low adhesive weight and over-large wheels, it was not practical for the gradients and doubtless Keeling intended rebuilding it as an 0—6—0ST.

On 8 September 1877 Keeling reported that 'a light locomotive belonging to our Company but not at present in use' had been let to Vickers & Cooke, the SBR contractors, at £14 per week. The only candidates were Nos. 2 and 3, and the 0—6—0, but Keeling had no need to describe Nos. 2 and 3 as 'belonging to our Company', and there is no evidence that either was out of use in 1877; compared with, say, *Friar Tuck*, the 0—6—0 was accurately described as light, and very suitable for the temporary track from Lydney to the Bridge. The locomotive returned at the end of 1879, was put to stock in 1880, and named *Ranger*. A typical day's work was to bank the first coal empties about 6.0 a.m. up to Moseley Green, returning to shunt at Lydney Jcn and Docks, banking as required thereafter.

Ranger has become celebrated as an 'obscure locomotive', but to the S & W it was a notorious 'white elephant' for the frequency of its derailments, possibly due to faulty balancing. At last it was converted to a saddle tank by Avonside in January 1891, with new cylinders and firebox. The 5-ft 1-in. wheels were not renewed or even re-tyred, for in 1892 they became really dangerous and fore-man Anderson had to order a new set at 4 ft 3 in. dia. from the Vulcan Foundry. Other fittings at this time were a steam brake and an LNWR whistle.

Ranger continued to shunt at Lydney and was seldom permitted out of sight with a train. The GWR could often make much out of little but could do nothing with *Ranger* except number it (1358, in September 1895). It was withdrawn in October 1896 and cut up at Swindon a year later, after a GWR mileage of only 17,413. GWR records state that in 1891 *Ranger* was altered from a combined tank and tender engine, but in 1952 two retired employees could recall

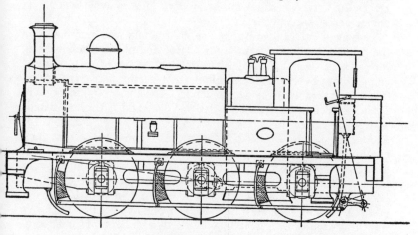

Ranger as a saddle tank

it, first as an ordinary tender engine, later as an 0—6—0ST without a tender, although the tender was included in returns until 1894.

HIRED AND SECOND-HAND ENGINES

In addition to *Hercules* three locomotives were hired from Boul-ton, all described and illustrated by Bennett in *The Chronicles of Boulton's Siding*. One was an 0—6—0ST built at Ashton about 1869 partly from scrap, with inside cylinders 15 in. x 24 in. and wheels 3 ft 6 in. dia. *Nelson*, a Thwaites & Carbutt 0—6—0 tender engine rebuilt by Boulton as a saddle tank, was far from satisfactory, and in December 1875 Keeling recommended that it be 'sent home' as he had inspected a six-wheeled (four-coupled) saddle tank at Bristol, offered by Llewellyn & James; he agreed to hire it, but probably did not do so, for in 1876 further assistance came from Boulton in the shape of *Queen*, an ex-LNWR Wolverton 0—6—0 goods engine of 1846, rebuilt as a saddle tank, with inside cylinders 15 in. x 24 in. and 3-ft 6-in. wheels; it was back at Ashton in 1881.

These machines must have been of limited use, probably on shunting and construction trains. Doubtless Keeling was pleased when the bridge was opened and he could send the last one 'home', henceforth all hired locomotives coming from the MR. By November 1879 Keeling had hired one at £2 per day, and the last recorded was Johnson 0—6—0T No. 1094 in 1894. In 1882 the Sharpness New Docks Co. agreed to shunt the S & W dock lines to avoid sending an engine across specially from Lydney.

Two locomotives used by the SBR contractors were purchased by the Amalgamation Committee for £1,300 and put to stock in 1880. *Raven*, an 0—6—0ST, was built by Boulton in 1876 as a 'new' engine, new by Boulton's standards that is; the basis was an ex-Great Northern Railway steam tender. The inside cylinders were 12 in. x 18 in., the wheels 3 ft 0 in. dia., and a Boulton patent water-tube boiler was fitted. In October 1876 *Raven* was sold for £1,100 to Vickers & Cooke, after the SBR had insisted that they employ a locomotive. *Raven* was chiefly used by the S & W on shunting and ballast duties, and about 1882 was hired daily to Foxes Bridge colliery; it would bank an early goods up the Mineral Loop, spend the day at the colliery and return light to Lydney in the evening. Keeling ordered a new boiler from Avonside in 1889, but *Raven* was withdrawn in 1892 and sold to a Mr Drew of Cinderford.

The 0—4—0 well-tank *Severn Bridge* was a Fletcher, Jennings 10 in. patent built in 1876 and purchased by Griffith, Griffiths & Co. in 1878. It was renamed *Wye* in 1880. *Wye* probably reminded Keeling of his first hard-won locomotives; not for this one the green livery, but a special maroon, lined yellow. Thus distinguished, it worked the engineer's inspection coach, and performed shunting and emergency goods and passenger work. In 1881 Colonel Rich objected to the use of four-wheeled locomotives on passenger trains, presumably having observed *Wye* thus engaged. It only had a hand brake on the trailing wheels, yet as late as 1894 ran 38 passenger miles. The goods duties were usually controlling trains down to Lydney, accompanied by much 'pinning down', and on occasion *Wye* could be seen creeping south with 40 or 50 wagons.

Keeling's coach was always propelled into the Forest, and as a special train was heralded by a red board on the back buffer beam of the preceding train. One hot summer day the young crossing-keeper at Travellers Rest failed to notice this board and went swimming in a nearby pool, to be startled by the imperious summons of *Wye's* whistle at his signal. He grabbed his trousers and ran, much to the driver's amusement, but apparently unnoticed by the great man in the coach.

Wye was repaired by E. Walker, late of the Avonside Engine Co., at Bristol in 1892. As built, *Wye* did not have the frail cab later carried, and may not have had side tanks.

THE VULCANS

In addition to *Ranger, Raven* and *Wye,* two new locomotives came from the Vulcan Foundry in 1880, for traffic was expected from the SBR and Keeling had suggested ordering at least one new locomotive, similar to *Friar Tuck.* Evidently the Vulcan salesman induced him to adopt the cranked axle, and he ordered an 0—6—0T at £1,820 to be delivered in only three months. *Sharpness* arrived in March 1880, followed on 28 April by *Severn Bridge* (on hire-purchase terms). The principal differences from previous locomotives were inside cylinders, Ramsbottom safety valves, and all-over cabs.

Sabrina (the Latin name for Severn) was delivered in July 1882, and *Forester* in June 1886. *Forester* was ordered on hire-purchase but apparently the company then discovered that a renewal need not be charged to capital but could be debited to revenue, so it was classed as a 'renewal' of the old locomotive sold some three years previously and was not 'declared' to the Board of Trade. This false return of 12 continued until the Joint Committee was formed, receiving 13 locomotives.

Finally came *Gaveller* in March 1891, the 18th and last locomotive, and the only one built with the vacuum brake. (The Gaveller was the Crown official responsible for the letting or galing of land for mining purposes and for collecting pit rents.) The Vulcans, well suited to the Forest, were the most useful of all the locomotives, one of them usually working the Coleford branch passenger train.

THE DRIVERS AND THEIR HEADQUARTERS

An engine house built of timber, with a workshop, was erected in 1865 for the five tramroad engines, on the present site, a place then known as Pill House in Church Road, Lydney, and in 1868 the committee agreed to lengthen it for the two broad-gauge engines expected. In 1876 three locomotive engineers, Appleby, Tomlinson and Fisher, called in to report on locomotives and maintenance staff, found that neither was equal to the traffic; they recommended an additional engine shed, to which the company agreed. In December 1879 Glover, the MR locomotive superintendent at Gloucester, was advising on improvements and in 1880 the company purchased 'the iron church at Cheltenham' for £150, placing it near Lydney GWR station—surely a unique transformation, for it was used as a carriage shed and for engine painting.

The fitting shop was entered from the rear by a line between the shed and the stores. Machinery was always in demand, and it was not until its last years that the company could effect major overhauls; even then, engines had sometimes to be sent to Avonside at considerable expense. In January 1877 two engines were 'sent to the shed' and the crews stood off until trade improved. However, good work was done at Lydney, including gauge alterations, cylinder boring, fitting of vacuum brakes and re-boilering.

In 1891 it became apparent that all was not well at Lydney depot. Following a report by Owen of the Brecon & Merthyr Railway, the locomotive foreman, Joseph Conquest, was pensioned and 'great blame was attached to the leading boilersmith'. The fireboxes had been badly neglected, but by mid-December they were in 'fair' condition. John Anderson of Glasgow became foreman in 1892, having worked for the North British Railway, Dübs & Co., and as locomotive superintendent of the Quebrada Railway, South America. He was capable and was ably assisted by his charge fitter, Crelling. After 1894 extensive repairs were no longer carried out at Lydney, the machinery was sold, and it soon became just an ordinary ill-equipped running shed repair depot.

Employees worked long hours and there were only 12 crews, each driver keeping to his own engine. Several drivers who joined the company in the middle 1860s were still driving in 1895 and the oldest was only 55 years old then. William ('Bob') Ridler started in 1865, was driving before 1870, and became the chief passenger driver, on *Maid Marian*. He thoughtfully made notes of various early locomotive matters. In April 1891 while *Maid Marian* was in the shops, Ridley was driving *Sabrina;* he was thrown off at Otterspool Jcn and seriously injured, but recovered at Gloucester Infirmary. In 1894 he was found 'under the influence' in charge of a passenger train but he survived this disgrace, although he had to forfeit his share of the yearly premium allocated to drivers for economical working. It was presented to his fireman with the explanation that the latter had done a good deal of driving during the year!

The brothers William and James Ellaway both joined the service in the 1860s. The former had *Will Scarlet* and was known as 'Uncle Locks' to the young 'spotters' of the period, who could often be seen on his engine while the fireman did the driving. James also enjoyed his glass and for a while was demoted to the canal dredger but finished his 30 years of service as a 'ballast driver' on either *Robin Hood* or *Wye*. Neither brother could write and the guards used to fill up the journals for them.

On *Severn Bridge* could be seen bearded, eccentric Tom Wellington, who used his many opportunities of making contacts wisely as an agent for Kendal & Dent, the watch manufacturers, and who composed a once-famous verse used in their advertisements, which earned him a gold ring. William Powell on *Alan-a-Dale* was the trade union man, equivalent of the modern shop steward, this being the era of the Amalgamated Society of Railway Servants and before the formation of the NUR. His brother Charles had *Friar Tuck*.

The livery of the early locomotives is not recorded; those used, from at least the '80s onwards, were defined by Mr Bracey as follows:

Standard Livery: Chinese Green, a shade midway between B.S. 5-064 and B.S. 5-065 of British Standard No. 2660:1955.

Wye: Wine or plum colour equivalent to B.S. 1-025 of B.S. 2660: 1955.

In both cases the lining was yellow.

PASSENGER ROLLING STOCK

In 1874 three composite and four third-class carriages were ordered at about £50 each from the Gloucester Wagon Co. on hire-purchase terms, and there was also a first-class of unknown origin. Three third-class carriages had brake compartments, and the stock was equipped with Clarke & Webb's patent continuous chain brakes, screw couplings and side chains. The second class was soon discontinued, from 1 December 1875.

In 1879 four coaches were in use, with three in reserve or repair, the eighth probably being used for inspection purposes. More carriages were required for the new Severn Bridge line, and the Bristol Wagon Co. delivered three composites at £226 each, and one third class, by January 1880. In 1884 passengers complained of the hard, uncushioned third-class seats as compared with those of the GWR and MR, and they were refurnished. The 'excursion or saloon carriage' required extensive repairs in 1889 and it was decided to use it as a brake van and obtain a replacement (possibly No. 12).

The brake gear consisted of a chain wound on a drum adjacent to one axle. On application, a friction clutch drove the drum from the axle, making the chain taut and applying the brakes. In the guard's compartment was a lever which was lifted and pinned in a rack. A wire rope from the lever passed along the top of the coach and into the engine cab—the brake coach was generally placed next to the engine for this reason. By regulations, the brake cord was to be fastened to the engine before the train was started, but in practice the guard usually operated the brake.

In 1890 four ex-Bristol Port Railway & Pier Co. composites, a third-class saloon and a passenger brake van were purchased, mainly for excursion traffic. One, used by G. W. Keeling as his inspection coach, had open-end platforms and replaced an earlier vehicle, which had one open end.

The vacuum brake gear was fitted at Lydney, under the supervision of a Swindon man, and was brought into general service on 20 May 1892. In 1895 the stock was divided as follows:

Description	GWR	MR
Compo. 1st & 3rd	Nos. 1, 5, 11, 13, 16	2, 10, 14
Brake compo. 1st & 3rd		6, 8
Brake thirds	3, 7, 9	4
Third class	15, 17	
Brake van	18	
Horse box	19	
Carriage truck	20	
First-class saloon		12

No. 12 was the 'plum', valued at £120, the others only ranging from £12 to £25. Nothing is known of the Midland's share; the GWR numbered five of theirs 1962 to 1966 but condemned them in February 1896. All coaches had four wheels and were painted light brown.

After 1895 stock was supplied jointly, and some years later the GWR provided ten four-wheeled coaches, while the MR supplied eight bogie coaches. Regulations of May 1906 stated that normally trains were to be formed with two brake thirds and a brake composite for Cinderford and Lydbrook, and one of each type for the Coleford branch. In 1893 a corrugated iron shed was erected at Lydney Town to stable the three carriages of the last train from the

Forest. This was removed about 1910 and the Junction shed (the 'iron church') in 1924.

GOODS VEHICLES

The traffic was largely mineral, and traders supplied their own wagons, but in 1870 Keeling had reluctantly to order a broad-gauge guard's van, for safety's sake, and the S & W became notorious for owning only one piece of rolling stock. Two 'break vans' were ordered in 1872 for the opening of the Loop line, and in 1874 wagons were hire-purchased to ensure a regular supply of Welsh locomotive coal. The Gloucester Wagon Co. supplied nearly all the rolling stock, but some came from the Bristol Wagon Co. The 62 goods vehicles were valued at £1,092, and divided between the joint owners in 1895; they were: open 37, coal 10, covered 5, cattle 2, goods brake vans 6, a breakdown van and a ballast wagon.

Brake vans were always scarce before 1895; if none was available a guard was required to ride on the last truck, but in practice there was sometimes a shortage of guards for this unenviable duty, and a tree bough was tied on, to notify the signalman that the train was complete. Until recent years breakdown vans, and a shunting truck used at Lydney Harbour, were supplied by the GWR but lettered 'S & W Joint' or 'Severn & Wye Joint Line'.

CHAPTER 11

Locomotives on the Severn & Wye Joint Railway

THE CHANGING SCENE AT LYDNEY DEPOT

The joint owners had difficulty in deciding how to operate the line, and at Paddington on 23 April 1895 the GWR suggested that the rolling stock should be taken over in equal proportions by the two companies, who would then supply locomotives. The MR thought that the stock should be retained and the line worked by the Joint Committee. At St Pancras on 22 July the first proposal was adopted, and the GWR agreed to provide locomotives for ten years at fixed charges.

No drastic changes took place at Lydney depot for at least a year after the railway became joint property. The S & W locomotives continued to work the traffic, sometimes assisted by an odd 'hireling'. Changes were taking place behind the scenes, however; early in 1895 Anderson was relieved of his post and a notice dated 15 May was posted at the shed:

> As a temporary arrangement . . . leading fitter J. Crelling will have charge of workshops. . . . He is to be on duty at 6.0 a.m. to take charge when the night foreman goes off duty and to leave at 6.0 p.m. On Sundays J. Crelling is to supervise the work being carried on by boilersmiths. . . . When an accident or breakdown occurs J. Crelling will take charge. . . .
>
> Timekeeper A. Clarke will take charge . . . of booking engines and drivers for the following day in accordance with the traffic requirements stated by Mr Lamb. . . .
>
> Both J. Crelling and A. Clarke will be directly responsible to Mr Keeling who is responsible for the efficient carrying on of the locomotive work.
>
> Retired foreman Conquest will assist Mr Keeling as Inspector in seeing that the work is properly carried on.
> > Signed
> > Geo. William Keeling.

The Joint Committee did not decide how to operate the line until July 1895 but clearly big changes were inevitable. Keeling had anticipated them, dispensing with Anderson and taking over the locomotive department himself. Poor Crelling must have had an unbearably busy life, working six days a week for 12 hours a day together with a Sunday turn, and going out on breakdowns, which occurred frequently at this time. 'Retired' foreman Conquest, politely sacked in 1891, returned with promotion.

By 21 October 1895 the locomotives had been valued at £9,240 and allocated to their owners (see Appendix). *Little John* had been rebuilt, hence the high value, but *Alan-a-Dale* and *Will Scarlet* needed renovation. *Gaveller* was quite new, *Severn Bridge* had been reboilered, and both were of considerable value. £500 for *Ranger* was a 'paper' value only.

The MR engines were maintained at Derby, and did not return. *Robin Hood* had never been extensively rebuilt, was worn out and must have been quickly cut up, having no Derby record. *Little John* was not much altered, and was broken up in 1905. *Friar Tuck* was rebuilt in 1895, the vacuum brake being removed, and was reduced to shunting. A new, slightly larger boiler was fitted, also MR chimney and details. *Sharpness* had 17-in. cylinders fitted in 1899, and a new boiler in 1908 of Johnson type as on *Friar Tuck*. The official photograph shows it as MR 1124A but with a Johnson boiler, which suggests that it was reboilered before 1908—probably in 1899; it was shunting at Toton in 1919 and was broken up in 1924. *Sabrina* was reboilered in 1895 and fitted with 17-in. cylinders in 1905. The vacuum brake was retained and for a while it worked on the Coaley branch train, being later at Burton-on-Trent. *Forester* also acquired an MR boiler in 1895, and 17-in. cylinders in 1914. It was at Burton-on-Trent in 1915 and 1921, and was the last S & W locomotive to remain in service, being broken up in December 1924.

The seven GWR locomotives were generally repaired at Swindon, but were used for some years at Lydney. From available photographs it appears that while the MR removed the nameplates, the GWR retained them, with the exception of *Wye*.

Alan-a-Dale and *Will Scarlet* were rebuilt in 1896. Swindon was building replacement boilers for the '517' class 0—4—2Ts, and two of these were shortened by 2 in. to fit; they had raised fire-boxes. New cylinders, side tanks, steam-operated cast iron brakes, and the vacuum brake were fitted, also a GWR chimney, brass dome cover, safety valves on the fire-box and a small Dean-type front cab. *Alan-a-Dale* was back at Lydney by November 1896, after 11 months at Swindon. It was soon derailed at Lydney and Wimberry, and between 1901 and 1904 was working at Newport.

The rebuilding of *Will Scarlet* was completed in August 1896, but it was midsummer 1897 before it returned to Lydney and it soon spent two days at Coleford, off the rails. It was at Worcester in 1903, Hereford in 1904, and Wrexham in 1908—1909; in May 1911 it was in Carmarthenshire working on the newly-opened Lampeter, Aberayron & New Quay Light Railway. In November 1912 it was sold to the Bute Works Supply Co. for £500 (£300 *more* than the estimated value of 1895), resold to the Alexandra (Newport & South Wales) Dock & Railway Co., which removed the name and numbered it 32, handing it back to the GWR in 1922. The number 1356 was cheerfully allotted again but not carried, and *Will* was scrapped in 1923 after 50 years' service.

Maid Marian soon lost the distinction of being *the* S & W passenger locomotive, but 15 in. x 22 in. Swindon cylinders had been fitted at Lydney in March 1895. It was on loan to the Sharpness New Docks Co. in 1896, at Newport in 1900, and at Swindon in 1904 for a new boiler, similar to the 1893 one. The *Maid* roamed down to St Blazey shed in Cornwall, where it stood little used, and at one period was spare engine for the Goonbarrow branch; the rigid wheel-base was too long for the curves, so for a while the trailing coupling rods were removed, but with even less success. The engine was repaired at Worcester before sale in March 1910 to Baldwins Ltd for £650. It went to their Bryn Navigation Colliery, near Maesteg, and was named *Victor*, being cut up early in 1920.

No extensive use was made by the GWR of *Severn Bridge* or *Gaveller*, both in good order. *Severn Bridge* was the last engine rebuilt at Lydney and was fitted with a Vulcan replacement boiler in 1895. Apparently the engine never left Lydney, being condemned at Swindon in October 1905. *Gaveller* was new in 1891 and only required repairs (Swindon 1896), being little changed apart from acquiring GWR details. *Gaveller* also remained at Lydney and was derailed in March 1899, the last reference in Lydney records to a S & W locomotive. It had run 121,554 miles for the S & W and was cut up in 1903 after a total mileage of only 218,596 and less than 13 years' service.

Wye was in fair condition; it was at Stafford Road, Wolverhampton, in November 1898 but was not repaired. In 1900 it was back in its old haunts, working for the contractor on the Cinderford extension together with his own locomotive. Apart from a spell on the Wantage Tramway in 1906 nothing else is known of *Wye*, and it was condemned in 1910. *Ranger* was soon disposed of, as already noted.

An S & W return summarises the locomotive duties in 1894; all 13 are listed, also MR 1094 and GWR 2011, the last two accounting for most of the hire charges. 1094 was the last MR locomotive stationed at Lydney. 2011, the first GWR locomotive to arrive, was one of 160 Wolverhampton-built 0—6—0STs with inside cylinders, completed in November 1894 and going new to Lydney. By 31 December, 2011 had completed 1,080 miles, mostly on passenger duties.

GWR REINFORCEMENTS ARRIVE

The MR (ex-S & W) locomotives were replaced by GWR Wolverhampton-built inside-cylinder 0—6—0Ts, including during 1896—1897 Nos. 634-38, 1024-36-42-54-75. The '633' class were side tanks built in the early 1870s and originally fitted with condensers for London Division duties; the '1016' class were saddle tanks with double frames and originated in 1867. In 1897 the first of the '2021' class 0—6—0STs were built at Wolverhampton and some (including 2021) went straight to Lydney, replacing the '633s' and '1016s'; with inside cylinders 16 in. x 24 in. and 4 ft 1½ in. dia. wheels they proved successful and held a monopoly of both passenger and goods trains for 50 years.

In one detail at least, all these GWR engines were inferior to some of the S & W types—they had open-back cabs affording little protection, and some remained thus until withdrawn in 1950. There were no less than 30 engine derailments, mostly at Lydney shed and docks, between 1897 and 1900, mostly of the '2021' class but including some ex-S & W engines.

G. W. KEELING

George William Keeling was born in 1839 and after schooling worked for Thomas E. Blackwell, engineer to the Kennet & Avon Canal and for Bristol Docks, who was first employed by the S & W in 1847, as a consultant. By 1854 Keeling was assisting his father in the company's office, and in 1856 he assisted Blackwell in reporting on the main drainage of London. Blackwell was appointed vice-president and general manager of the Grand Trunk Railway, Canada in 1857, and Keeling, 18 years old, completed the supervision of the S & W works in progress. He was appointed inspector of the works at £60 p.a. from 29 March 1857 and was designated engineer in 1860. Keeling had the executive responsibility for the introduction of locomotives, of the broad gauge, and for the reconstruction of the system; he was particularly busy in 1872 with the Severn Bridge, the s & w extensions, assisting Clegram with Sharpness Docks and surveying the MR Sharpness Branch. In 1873 he married Miss C. Vivian of Cornwall, and was elected a member of the Institution of Civil Engineers. Keeling succeeded his father as general manager from 1879 until 1894, when he again took charge of the locomotive department, later succeeding J. W. Armstrong as superintendent engineer of the Gloucester and Hereford Divisions, GWR. It was in this capacity that Keeling was seriously injured on 5 February 1903.

Keeling left Gloucester at 7.35 a.m. to inspect the s & w with a friend, Lockett, and the clerk of the works, Scholes, the inspection coach being hauled by an 0—4—2T, class '517', running chimney first. After inspecting Lydney Docks they were joined by a surveyor and proceeded north, delayed by heavy traffic, until at Drybrook Road Keeling decided to omit Cinderford and return via the Mineral Loop, to inspect a new overbridge at Foxes Bridge.

The Loop was operated without the benefit of any recognised system, signals or telegraph; trains could, and did, enter it from both ends. On this morning the 6.30 a.m. Loop freight from Lydney, engine 2032, having reached Drybrook Road, returned to Foxes Bridge for a further load, also to be worked out via Drybrook Road. Porter-signalman Ellaway overlooked this, for at 12.25 p.m. he allowed the special to enter the section without warning the driver. The freight guard knew nothing about the special and started back, the trains meeting head-on at low speed near Crump Meadow, the trees and curves having masked them from each other. The enginemen all jumped clear but the unsuspecting officials were thrown from their armchairs and knocked unconscious. Keeling was standing on the observation platform with his back to a large glass window, through which he was thrown backwards. The 0—4—2T was damaged and derailed. An engine and brake van commandeered from a ballast train hurried Keeling and the surveyor to Lydney, where a doctor joined the train, and it ran through to Cheltenham. Keeling's skull had been fractured and he did not recover consciousness until the next day.

Evidence given at the enquiry reveals the then lively scene at Drybrook Road. In addition to the Loop coal train and the special, Ellaway had a Cinderford—Lydbrook passenger train approaching, a coal train in Trafalgar siding and a ballast train in the station loop —small wonder that the porter-signalman was regraded to signalman in 1904, as he spent 10 hours daily in the box.

Keeling retired from railway service on 30 September 1904. Appropriately enough, his last recorded task was reporting on the condition of the Severn Bridge. He had been appointed consulting engineer for the Sharpness New Docks and Gloucester & Birmingham Navigation Co. in 1885, and was later chairman and engineer on the harbour and pilotage boards. He was joint engineer to the Severn Commission and as a consultant engineer he practised in London with a partner.

The family left Lydney in the 1890s and settled at 10 Lansdown Terrace, Cheltenham. Keeling had been made a J.P. in 1889 and continued to serve on both the Lydney and the local benches; for over 20 years he was churchwarden at Christ's Church, Cheltenham, and was also treasurer of the Cotswold Convalescent Home and a member of the Bristol & Gloucestershire Archæological Society. He died on 21 June 1913, aged 74, and no less than 60 papers as far away as Belfast, Dundee, East Anglia and Yorkshire carried obituaries. As engineer, churchman or magistrate he exhibited sound judgment combined with quiet decision. Mrs Keeling also died in 1913 but members of the family lived at Lansdown Terrace until 1955.

LATER LOCOMOTIVE DEVELOPMENTS

Under the agreement of 1895 the GWR was to supply engine power for ten years; this agreement was renewed and ultimately covered the span of joint ownership to 31 December 1947.

In 1913, 20 of the '2021' class 0—6—0STs were stationed at Lydney. During the first world war Dean's 0—6—0 tender engines were first allocated to Lydney for working a through train of Forest coal to Taunton *via* the Severn Bridge; this 'double home' turn alternating with Taunton continued to run until June 1932, after which the Lydney engine ran only as far as Stoke Gifford. These were the first tender engines at Lydney, other than *Ranger*. In 1912 the GWR had commenced replacing the saddle tanks of the '2021' class with pannier tanks, but the first Lydney engine to be so treated was 2149, in 1923.

In 1926, for economy, it was proposed to use 2—6—2Ts on certain freight trains. They would have been a big advance in power, but the engineers required £50,000 to strengthen the line— the equivalent of five of the 'King' class then under construction. On 23 March 1931 Bullo Pill shed was closed and certain duties were transferred to Lydney, including the FOD branch passenger trains. For this, Lydney acquired a new 0—4—2T in June 1933 (No. 4813) and one or more were thereafter stationed there.

The GWR had never used 'push-pull' auto trains on the Joint line, but on and from 30 November 1936 the surviving service was operated by them, primarily to avoid fouling the level crossing by running round at Lydney Town. At first, auto fitted '2021' engines were used, but by 1938 a second 0—4—2T was provided and thereafter the '2021s' were only used when the 0—4—2Ts were under repair. An improved 0—6—0PT of the '74XX' class was stationed at Lydney during 1937—1938 for working the short-lived 9.50 p.m. Lydney to Ebbw Jcn goods train.

World war two saw the '2021s' still monopolising freight duties, but replacement became imminent as some were 50 years old. A new design of 0—6—0PT appeared from Swindon to replace them generally, of very similar dimensions; the first (1616) arrived at Lydney late in 1949 and thereafter replacement was rapid. The first of the '54XX' class, 0—6—0PT, 5417, arrived at Lydney on 22 March 1951 while No. 2080 yet lingered there, one of two '2021' engines temporarily fitted with larger wheels 20 years previously, as prototypes for the '54XX' series in 1931. The '54XXs' were used on the Cinderford and Berkeley Road passenger services. No. 2080 was the last of its class to leave, going to Swindon for scrapping on 26 March 1952. It was auto-fitted (as were 2102-32-58, its stable companions), and had done some passenger working.

No. 6341, a 2—6—0 which arrived in April 1952, was the first outside-cylinder engine stationed at Lydney since the departure of the 'natives' 50 years before. In July it was tried on the Coleford branch, but failed twice with trains, the combination of large wheels, steep gradient and sharp curves proving too much. It was, however, used to replace the 'Deans' on the Stoke Gifford coal trains. Early in 1953 one of the '56XX' 0—6—2Ts was tried on the Coleford branch with more success but none were put to work at Lydney, the Coleford trains being worked usually by '57XX' or '16XX' engines, frequently double-headed.

In April 1960 the Lydney allocation was 20 crews and 14 locomotives, all 0—6—0T (mainly '16XX' class) except for a 2—6—0, an 0—6—0, and an 0—4—2T. By early 1965 the '16XX' class had all left the district, and '57XX' tank engines were in charge of all normal traffic, although at that time a Collett 0—6—0 was reported as making a trip to Coleford, and a 2—6—0 venturing to Milkwall on a breakdown train, to re-rail a van on the Sling branch, itself suffered a derailed pony truck. (See Appendix 1 for later events at Lydney.)

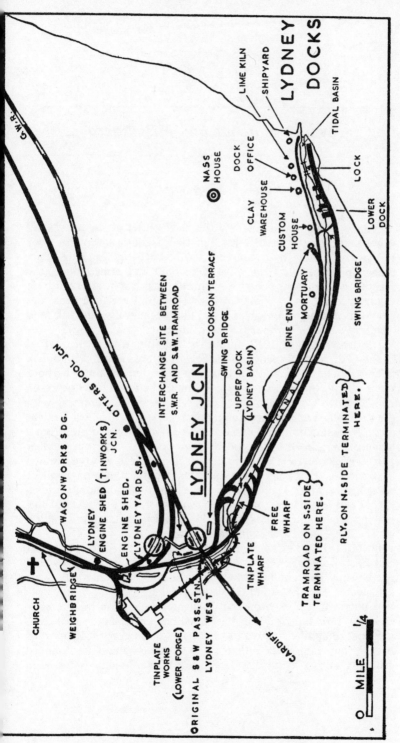

Map No. 8. Lydney Jcn and Docks

CHAPTER 12

Lydney Harbour and Miscellanea

THE SOUTHERN OUTLET

Lydney harbour was for long the chief outlet of the s & w, and although now little used it has functioned continuously for over 150 years. Lydney town, a mile from the harbour, was long established; in the 1650s large ships were built and armed there, the Severn then running near the church, but soon afterwards it changed course, leaving the town well inland. By 1800 a canal ran down to Lydney Pill owned by the ironmasters Pidcock and Homfray[1], but no harbour had been built.

The s & w Act of 1810 authorised a basin, to include part of Lydney Pill, a canal thence to the Severn at Nass Point, with a lock to an outer harbour, and a pair of tide gates, but the outer harbour work was postponed due to lack of funds. The canal was opened on 17 March 1813, five decorated boats with passengers entering with the flood tide, and another coming from Berkeley Pill.[2] Coal brought down by tramroad had, however, been shipped long before, from a 'temporary railroad by the side of Lydney Pill' existing in October 1810. The waterfront at the basin was divided into wharves, rented by traders so that they could build up stocks without payment of wharfage. Samuel Hayward of Little Dean was appointed lock-keeper at 15s per week, with leave to carry on his business of shoe-making when not wanted at the lock, and in spite of the modest wage a £500 bond was required of him.

In July 1813, to establish a trade westward to Chepstow, Newport and Bristol, the s & w followed Newport's example, and allowed a gratuity to masters of vessels so loading. Other markets were Bridgwater, Minehead and the Channel Isles.

A duty was imposed on coal brought into London by sea, after the great fire, and from this developed one on sea-borne coal from one port to another, which lost the s & w promoters the support of Bristol, but they hoped that as their trade would be confined generally to the Severn they would secure exemption.

L

In 1814 the Treasury declined to establish a customs officer at Lydney, and the s & w turned to smuggling; a Mr Champion of Bristol induced them to purchase a trow for £70, and 30 tons of coal, which they tried to land in that city free of duty. Unfortunately Bristol *had* a customs officer who, after his kind, stubbornly refused the freebooters permission to land the coal without paying duty; they returned disconsolate to Lydney, and sold the trow and coal. The Park End Coal Co. had their own method of beating the duty. Aust Pill (on the south bank of the Severn) was the boundary for the Ports of Gloucester and Bristol. Coal was landed on the Pill in the Port of Gloucester, carted over a bridge, and shipped again to Bristol; as it had not been *shipped* from one port to another it was free of duty.

There were many attempts to secure exemption, including an s & w petition of 1823 to Parliament, which stated that the undertaking had reduced the price of coal in the district by 50-80 per cent, greatly benefiting the public, but reaping little corresponding reward, as the duty excluded traders from Chepstow, Bristol and Bridgwater. The Duty Acts were not repealed generally until 1833.

Unusual tides, and shifting sand bars which were sometimes two feet higher than the tide-gate sill, made pilots necessary. The company's pilot boat was lost in a winter's gale, in 1816—1817, while in 1821 a new six-oar tow boat was purchased to assist vessels down the river. Certificates were issued to qualified pilots in 1823, after a schooner had been lost due to unskilled efforts, but some of them were rugged fellows and in 1825 Sheasby complained that Richard Sinderby had caused damage 'by running vessels against the wall of the outer harbour, and had also been very abusive when spoken to'; his yearly certificate was not renewed.

The outer harbour was completed in October 1821 and Sheasby extended the tramroad thence from the basin along the north side of the canal, a branch across to a new wharf on the west side of the harbour being added in 1823. Bathurst's wharves and warehouses were thereby rendered less important and the company secured an Act on 24 June 1822[3], authorising payment to him of compensating royalties. The trade westward, and to Thames markets, increased immediately, and in January 1822 Captain John Propert of the brig *Minerva* was given £12 for 'his great exertions in promoting a trade to the Westward', although the company would not compensate him for his earlier exertions in damaging his vessel whilst loading at the uncompleted outer harbour. The entrance was badly positioned as vessels of over 12-ft draught could only enter on spring tides.

In 1824 it was discovered that the coal used by the lock-keeper for 'fires for the lamps of the Company' and for his private use, was obtained 'without being purchased', a fact which could not have dimmed the cheerful welcome of the flaming braziers to vessels venturing in at night.

Lydney harbour suffered from a shortage of water in times of drought, the Severn silt aggravated the nuisance, and continuous war was waged on the twin evils by the s & w engineer. The mud was removed, at first by hand, emptying the canal, and after 1847 by hiring a dredger. A steam dredger was provided for the harbour in 1871, and another in 1879 for the canal. By the 1880s steamboats had become more numerous, and due to the inadequacy of the lock the bigger vessels, unable to pass through, had to be loaded in the small tidal basin, causing obstruction. Traffic was being lost to Bullo Pill, but it was not until 1890 that two steam pumps (asked for by G. W. Keeling in 1866) were ready for use, at the outer harbour, to maintain the water level.

CHINA CLAY, SALT AND BOAT-BUILDING

By 1822 a trade in china clay had been established, brought back in lieu of ballast, no doubt from Cornish ports, and to encourage cleanliness in its re-shipment to the Potteries, Sheasby erected two stages beside the canal, above the outer harbour, with a movable stage to the vessels. The clay warehouse was derelict by 1846.

Robert Withy of Howlers Slade colliery, in conjunction with the Droitwich Salt Co., erected a salt warehouse near the lock in 1825, and in 1832 adjacent land was granted to the Patent Salt Co. of Droitwich for salt works and a dock, but the trade had apparently ceased by 1848.

A barge and boat-building yard was established by David Davies to the south of the basin in 1834, but being an impediment to the canal trade was given up in favour of one at the outer harbour. The last boat was built in 1937, but the tiny slipway can still be seen.

In 1853 the s & w was refused powers to enlarge the canal and harbour but in 1862 it applied again, and also sought a branch from the South Wales line down the west side of the canal. The Board of Trade frowned upon the proposal to double the harbour charges for coal not coming down the tramroad, and the bill was withdrawn. In December 1866 a curve was proposed from the South Wales line to Pill House (near the locomotive shed) and thence to the upper basin, using one broad-gauge rail and one combined rail and tramplate, and this may well have been done—it would explain the limited purchase of combined plates. In 1867 Lydney was handling coal, pig iron, bark, timber and paving stone.[4] Nearly 200 vessels, of 20 to 400 tons, were employed, handling over 200,000 tons yearly.

The directors inspected the wharves, and the new railway and tips at the outer harbour, on 22 May 1872. The old wharves were on both sides of the basin, each with a 'fan' of tramroad sidings and a small tip, but in due course a few comparatively large s & w tips replaced them.

In 1897 Lydney loaded 265,000 tons, and the nine coal tips and three cranes were kept busy. During and after the great war, trade was brisk, but later, with collieries failing rapidly, it declined, and in 1927 tips Nos. 1 and 2, for small vessels at the top of the canal, were dismantled.

The only development for many years in Lydney harbour was the establishment of the Pine End plywood works, to which one of the sidings in front of Cookson Terrace was extended in about 1940, but without connection to the harbour. On and from 1 January 1950 control of the harbour was transferred from the Railway Executive, B.T.C., to the Docks Executive, followed on 13 August by the transfer of railways and works. A dwindling coal trade continued in fairly recent years to Ilfracombe, Combe Martin, Minehead and Bristol, and once a year to the Scilly Isles, but the outer-harbour tips, and the railway to them, were closed on 18 November 1960, all track on the south side of the canal being removed in mid-1962.

The short stone pier juts out into the river, with the harbour-master's office and other reminders of the busy days contributing now to a tranquil charm. Derelict barges line the south side of the harbour, whilst at the upper basin a building dating from 1813 provides a link with the earliest days.

LYDNEY LEVEL CROSSING

The tramroad had been established for 35 years when the first proposals were made for the South Wales Railway. A bridge would have required expensive embankments, so in 1848 a level crossing was under discussion; G. B. Keeling and Blackwell met Brunel in 1851, and agreed that its laying was not to interfere with trade for more than one day, and was to commence on the night of May 30. The cost of interchange tramroad sidings was to come out of the swr 'settlement' of 1847 but a crane and intermediate platform were to be erected at joint cost.

SEVERN & WYE & SEVERN BRIDGE RAILWAY.

FOREST OF DEAN.

Excursions, Pleasure Parties, &c., to Severn Bridge, Speech House, Lydbrook (Symonds' Yat), &c.

During the Summer Months Excursion Tickets at low fares are issued on certain Week Days (see Bills) from Midland Stations at Cheltenham, Gloucester, Bristol and Bath, to Severn Bridge, Speech House, and Lydbrook.

Cheap Return Tickets will be issued to Pleasure Parties on any day for not less than Six First Class or Ten Third Class Passengers.

An attractive Guide to the Forest of Dean has been published by Mr. JOHN BELLOWS, Gloucester, and may be had of all Booksellers.

Special Arrangements at Cheap Fares can be made for Schools, Benefit Societies, Working Men's Clubs, or Manufacturers' Annual Trips, &c.

Near the Severn Bridge Station there is Hotel accommodation and Tea Gardens overlooking the River and the Severn Bridge.

The Speech House (within a few minutes' walk of the Station) is situated on a hill in the centre of the ancient forest, and is a most attractive place for pleasure parties.

Every accommodation can be provided by the Hotel in the Speech House, or for Picnics in the open forest, and there are Cricket, Quoit, Archery, and Lawn Tennis Grounds.

Telegraphic communications to Speech House, address via Lydney.

Lydbrook is beautifully situated on the River Wye amidst charming scenery.

Symonds' Yat and Goodrich Castle are within easy walking distance from the Lydbrook Junction Station, and tickets to that Station are available to return from Coleford Station, or *vice versa*.

A Picnic Carriage for Parties of about a dozen can be provided on application to the General Manager, Lydney. The charge for the carriage, in addition to the first class fares, is one guinea, which includes use of Dinner & Tea Services, Plate, Glass, Linen, and Attendant. The Carriage can be left, as desired, on Sidings near picturesque points of the forest, viz., Coleford Junction, Bixslade, Speech House Road, Serridge Junction, Drybrook Road, Lydbrook Junction.

GEO. WILLIAM KEELING,
Engineer & General Manager.

s & w advertisement in the *Handbook of Stations*, 1890

The gates were normally to be closed across the SWR, and opened at least five minutes before an SWR train was due; if it was more than ten minutes overdue, S & W traffic could proceed but a train was to take precedence over tram-wagons if both approached simultaneously. Gates, and disc and crossbar signals, were to be controlled by the SWR; the disc showing (or a white light) meant gates open, and the crossbar (red light), gates shut.

The SWR line was opened in 1851, and within a few months interchange facilities had been provided, including an S & W 'shelter box or office' for the convenience of traders, while in 1853 a new and larger SWR passenger station was built. Paddington was customarily high-handed with small neighbours, and the S & W had already crossed its path metaphorically, by opposing conversion of the FOD line. Consequently the company had to remind Paddington from time to time that *it* had obliged at Lydney, and not *vice versa*. On 19 April 1862 an up express train drawn by the engine *Leopard* left the rails, killing one person. A Lydney inquest jury suspected the gradient and the company authorised the SWR to raise the tramroad level at the crossing by about a foot.

The S & W broad-gauge line was extended to the harbour in 1870, and a third rail was laid in 1872 to take traffic from the standard-gauge Mineral Loop. The remaining tramroad track was replaced by a railway line in 1879, but this was removed in 1908, being little used. New crossing regulations of 1879 were still on the basis that, generally, the gates were to be open for S & W trains, thus recognising their seniority. The harbour railways were worked as a station yard, signals only being provided for the GWR level crossing and the swing bridge carrying the harbour line over the canal feeder.

EXCURSION TRAFFIC

The company went to considerable lengths to attract tourists to the Forest, and made special arrangements for pleasure parties. S & W posters were exhibited throughout the South, Bellows's guidebook, *A Week's Holiday in the Forest of Dean*, received an S & W royalty from 1884 until 1903, and excursion trains were run in conjunction with neighbouring railways. An advertisement in the 1890 *Handbook of Stations* summarised the facilities, including 'a Picnic Carriage' for hire with an attendant; it could be left as desired on picturesque sidings, and must surely have been the precursor of the camping coach.

In addition to normal excursions, special trains were run for such occasions as temperance and miners' demonstrations, Cinderford Eisteddfod, music contests near Walford Halt, steamers from Sharpness, and the Festival of Britain. The Lydbrook line rarely saw excursions, whereas Coleford was specially favoured. There were fewer excursions in post-war years, but some were run from Parkend.

'MIXED' TRAINS

As early as 1878 mixed goods and passenger trains were run, but Board of Trade authority was not obtained until 1900. They were limited to 25 vehicles, passenger carriages being in the front, and a brake van in the rear; the average running speed was not to exceed 25 m.p.h. Regulations of 1906 prohibited the 'habit' of sending ladders, poles, etc., by attaching them to carriage steps, in view of heavy gradients and curves, and carriages were then being fitted with a 'passenger chain'. Ticket money reached Lydney stationmaster in travelling cash safes on the last passenger trains each evening.

MIDLAND RAILWAY TRAINS TO COLEFORD

On 8 September 1879 at Derby, the Keelings, Lucy and Allport agreed that some S & W and MR trains should run to Berkeley Road and Lydney Jcn respectively. Some S & W trains soon did so and it is probable that certain MR trains worked to Lydney Jcn. Later the MR ran a four-coach train from Gloucester to Parkend, arriving about 10.0 a.m. and departing about 1.0 p.m., having been stabled at Coleford Jcn. Two S & W coaches from Coleford were attached to its rear, and detached at Lydney Jcn. This working was probably introduced in August 1888, when MR engines were taking water at Lydney and Parkend. This suggests tank engines, but by 1889 a 4—2—2 tender engine was used. In October 1891 the MR train from Gloucester leaving Berkeley Road at 4.2 p.m. was running to Coleford, returning thence at 6.10 p.m. Worked by an MR 0—4—4T, it ran until 1895, the earlier train being withdrawn. MR 0—4—4Ts Nos. 1280 and 1281 were used on Gloucester—Lydney trains via the Severn Bridge in this period.[5]

PERMANENT WAY

The original standard-gauge iron rails, of Vignoles type, 72 lb. per yd, purchased from the Plymouth, Dowlais and Aberdare ironworks at about £6 per ton, were laid partly in chairs and partly 'with clips to the sleepers'. In 1873, 500 tons of 'Steely iron top rails' (£11 10s per ton) were ordered from Aberdare for the Lydbrook line.

These rails proved unsuitable for heavy mineral traffic, and from 1877 onwards about 2 miles were replaced by steel rails annually. By 1879 the GWR standard double-headed steel rail had been adopted. In 1885 there were still 8½ miles of 'iron road', as Keeling called it, including the Coleford branch, which was soon relaid, and the last iron rails on the main line, through Upper Lydbrook station, were replaced in 1890. Coleford station, c 1920, boasted a length of track laid with flat-bottom rails marked 'Indian State Railways'.

In more recent years concrete padstone sleepers linked by tie-bars have been laid at various points, making an interesting contrast with the tramroad blocks, while the Drybrook Road loop was spiked through flat sole plates at every other sleeper, believed to be the original S & W form. Chairs marked 'GW & GCJt R' and dated 1903 were in use at Mierystock in 1955.

THROUGH MR AND GWR GOODS TRAINS

After 1894 the MR continued to run daily goods trains from Sharpness to Bristol and Gloucester, and for a long but indeterminate period one ran to Lydney Jcn with MR engine and crew. These trains continued to run after 1923, but soon after 1945 the Bristol train was withdrawn.

In 1906 the Joint Committee considered the running of through GWR coal trains over the Severn bridge, but this was not practicable until 1908, when the Westerleigh and Berkeley loops were opened, avoiding reversal. The running of these trains on Saturday nights over the MR from Yate, the Berkeley loop and the S & W was proposed. None were running in 1912, but in May 1914 there was a 7 p.m. GWR goods, Sharpness Docks to Gloucester via Lydney, and an 11.30 p.m. (when required), Lydney to Taunton via Berkeley Loop. In 1917 there were through trains from Sharpness to Stoke Gifford, Lydney Jcn to Taunton and to Weston-super-Mare, with balancing empty workings, and in September one was put on each way, Cardiff to Newton Abbot. In 1919 through up trains were: Lydney Jcn to Stoke Gifford, and to Taunton; Sharpness, Cardiff and Beachley to Stoke Gifford, and stone empties from Beachley to Yate, with balancing workings. The Stoke Gifford to Beachley train ran with two engines and vans to Sharpness, and was divided there, one taking stone to Beachley works, the other empties to Lydney. From this wartime peak the workings were gradually reduced, until latterly only one ran each way, Lydney Jcn to Stoke Gifford, and this was terminated by the Severn Bridge accident.

WHERE ONCE THE RAILS SHONE

The tramroads can still generally be followed, often with ease, but the last vestiges of iron-work (mile-posts, rails, etc.) have mostly disappeared (generally into better care than Nature affords), and the Forest scrub and plantations quickly claim back the way itself, where it is not used as a footpath or 'ride'. The closed railways have also been removed effectively, leaving for the most part only earthworks, but these can easily be followed.

The 1971 position is summarised in Appendices 1 and 2; in spite of the eradication of station and other buildings, lifting of surplus tracks, and change of motive power, it seems certain that, if the last railway in the Forest survives, it will continue to exhibit the distinctive character developed through one-and-a-half centuries of history.

Acknowledgments

This account is the first fruit of an investigation begun in 1949, after reading Mr T. B. Peacock's essays on the Coleford and Wye Valley lines. Contact was soon made with two confirmed Dean enthusiasts, Mr L. E. Copeland and Mr (now Rev) D. A. Tipper, who formed with the writer the group known as 'Dean Forester'. Mr Copeland brought to the group a detailed record of many sources, and prepared the large-scale maps reproduced here. Mr Tipper wrote the locomotive chapters and commissioned the painting used as the frontispiece. These two good friends also largely built up the photographic record, and I trust that they will feel that their labours are rewarded in this book.

Three former railway officials rendered great assistance. The late Mr T. E. R. Morris went to Cinderford as stationmaster in 1925; in 1931 he wrote articles on the Forest Tramroads in the *Locomotive Magazine*; he retired in 1946 as stationmaster at Ross-on-Wye. The late Mr M. Bracey spent the whole of his career on the s & w, commencing as 'lad porter' at Parkend in 1889, retiring as Chief Inspector, s & w Joint Railway, in 1938. Mr G. Hale commenced at Lydney locomotive depot in 1907 and was foreman clerk on his retirement in 1954.

Valuable assistance, here gratefully acknowledged, was also received from many other people, including Messrs B. Baxter, T. Bright, W. A. Camwell, R. Dagley-Morris, C. Hadfield, C. E. Hart, E. Hicks, S. H. P. Higgins, E. Hughes, the late Miss E. Keeling, Messrs Levett, the late W. McGowan Gradon, J. Marshall, J. E. Nicholls, J. E. Norris, E. S. Parker, K. P. Plant, Mrs D. Pope, Messrs A. Pope, P. J. T. Reed, E. S. Tonks, K. W. Allford and R. M. Huxley.

The company minute books, made available by the archivist of the British Transport Commission, have been drawn upon so freely that individual references to them are not given; they have provided the major source for matters of history. Much useful material has also been derived from the House of Lords' Record Office, Patent Office Library, Guildhall Library, Gloucester County Records Office and Deputy Gaveller's Office.

Mr David St John Thomas counselled wisely in the task of reducing the original rambling text to a manageable and more

co-ordinated form, while Mr C. R. Clinker provided valuable com-
ment and corroboration in certain matters of detail. My wife
gave continuous support in a task, the end of which must often
have seemed chimerical, and my sister, Miss F. E. Paar, typed the
manuscript through several drafts.

ILLUSTRATIONS

I acknowledge with gratitude permission to use photographs
from the cameras or collections of the following: Mr B. Baxter
(Nos. 4, 5), British Railways, LMR (21), Mr W. A. Camwell (28), Mr
L. E. Copeland (13, 20, 26, 30, 32-37), Mr T. J. Edginton (15), Sir
Arthur Elton (7), The Editor, *The Engineer* (17), The English Electric
Company Ltd (22), The Gloucester Railway Carriage & Wagon
Company Ltd (10), The Gloucestershire Newspapers Ltd (38, 39),
S. H. P. Higgins (2), Locomotive & General Railway Photographs
(18), Mr H. J. Patterson Rutherford (11, 14), Rev D. A. Tipper (1, 2,
3, 6, 8, 9, 12, 16, 23, 24, 25, 27, 29, 31).

The Stephenson Locomotive Society kindly made available blocks
for Nos. 23 and 24.

Text illustrations were made available as follows: 1839 bye-law
(p.65) and Section through track (p.120)—B.T.C. Archives; Gradient
Profiles (p.80)—Mr L. E. Copeland; s & w advertisement (p.150)—
Mr C. R. Clinker; 'Robin Hood'—*The Engineer*.

The large-scale area maps in the text are based upon the Ordnance
Survey Map, are reproduced with the sanction of the Controller of
H.M. Stationery Office, and the Crown Copyright is reserved.

All other illustrative material is from the author's collection.

H. W. Paar.

Chigwell, Essex.
1971.

References

Notes to Chapter 1 (*page* 13)

1. H. G. Nicholls, *The Forest of Dean*, 1858 (also the source for the condition of the roads).
2. Extract dated 1807 from the *Journal of the Proceedings to obtain the Forest Railway*, kept by the 'Gentlemen of Herefordshire'. In Bledisloe papers, Gloucestershire County Records, Ref. E.49.
3. Bledisloe papers, Ref. E.48.
4. *Gloucester Journal*, 12 October 1801.
5. 'Mr. Teague's Railway', described in Vol. 2.
6. From various letters, etc., in the Public Record Office, Ref. Treasury T.1.-883.
7. These plans are preserved, P.R.O., Ref. MPD 15, MPD 57.
8. Report in P.R.O., Ref. Treasury T.1.-883.
9. *Gloucester Journal*, 27 December 1802.
10. *Report and Estimate of the Proposed Rail-ways from the collieries . . . to the Rivers Severn and Wye*, Benjamin Outram, 1801. Bledisloe papers, Ref. D.421.
11. John Hodgkinson was the engineer of several tramroads in this part of the country, including the Hay Railway, contemporary with the Severn & Wye.
12. Letters from Thomas Tovey, solicitor of Newnham, dated 16 Jan. and 19 Sept. 1802. Bledisloe papers, Ref. D.421.
13. *Journal of the Proceedings* . . . etc. The writer has in fact found no evidence to suggest that the opposition originated from Glenbirvie—he probably acted in accordance with the advice of his local officers.
14. Fourth Report of the Dean Forest Commissioners, 25 August 1835, Appendix 1.
15. The Bullo Pill Railway, described in Vol. 2.
16. John Rennie's report to Lord Robert Spencer, British Transport Commission Historical Records, Ref. HRP1/31.
17. Described in Vol. 2.
18. Fourth Report of the Dean Forest Commissioners, 1835.
19. *Case of the Opponents to a Fourth Railway*, in B.T.C. Hist. Rec., Ref. HRP1/31.
20. In the House of Lords' Record Office.

Notes to Chapter 2 (*page* 20)

1. S & WR & C Act, 50 Geo. III, c. 215.
2. *Gloucester Journal*, 8 Jan. 1810.
3. Ibid. 21 May 1810.
4. Ibid.
5. S & WR & C Act, 51 Geo. III, c. 193.
6. Copy in B.T.C. Hist. Rec., Ref. HRP1/31.

7. Circular to the Proprietors of the S & WR & C Co. from David Mushet, one of the Committee of Management. Copy in S & W Minute Books.
8. 17 March was the actual opening day (see Chapter 12).
9. S & WR & C Act, 54 Geo. III, c. 42.
10. For an excellent account, see the *Railway Magazine*, May and Nov. 1947, 'The Abergavenny—Hereford Tramroads', by E. H. Morris.
11. Gloucester City Library: Catalogue of the Gloucester Collection, Ref. 2985.
12. In B.T.C. Hist. Rec., Ref. HRP1/31.
13. *The Forester* newspaper, 16 Dec. 1875 (from which is largely drawn also the description of the Coleford branch opening—Chapter 7).
14. The Minute Books refer to him as 'Mr Jessop, Junior', but he was probably Josias—the younger William seems to have devoted his time largely to the Butterley Company, following his father there.
15. Some further biographical information appears in *The Canals of South Wales and the Border*, 1960, by Charles Hadfield. Chapter 9 gives a good short account of the S & W, of particular use on the financial aspects, and the relationship with other transport facilities in the area.

Notes to Chapter 3 (page 29)

1. Information marked on a map of the system (dated 1853) sent to Gooch in 1856, when he was asked to advise on locomotives. In B.T.C. Hist. Rec., Ref. HL/1/1/9.
2. In the *Railway Magazine*, Nov. 1899.
3. B.T.C. Hist. Rec., Ref. HL/1/1/9.
4. T. E. R. Morris, articles, 'The Forest of Dean Tramroads', in *Locomotive, Railway Carriage and Wagon Review*, 1931.
5. In his paper, *Minutes to be observed in the Construction of Railways*, quoted in *Margaret Outram, 1778—1863*, by M. F. Outram, 1932.

Notes to Chapter 4 (page 44)

1. *The Forester* newspaper, August 1877.
2. Details of these Crown Licences will be found in the various Reports of the Commissioners of Woods & Forests, and some plans survive in the Deputy Gaveller's (now N.C.B.) office in Coleford.
3. Report of Collieries, Works and Railways, 1841. Glos. Co. Rec., Ref. Q/RUM/175.
4. Minutes of Evidence, Select Committee of the House of Commons on Woods, Forests and Land Revenues, 1848.
5. Information handed down in the family of Mr James Russell, whose father and grandfather both worked on the tramroads. Mr C. E. Lee has commented that an easier way to avoid the reduced rate and junction charges imposed by the Acts of Parliament concerned would have been to haul the wagons along a few yards of roadway between the unconnected lines. Further reference to this subject is made in Vol. 2.
6. See *The Story of the Mushets*, by F. M. Osborn, 1952.
7. Minutes of Evidence, Coleford Railway bill, 1872.
8. These alignments are shown on the deposited plans for the S & W Act, 1872.
9. Minutes of Evidence and deposited plans, Coleford Railway bill, 1872.

10. *A Week's Holiday in the Forest of Dean*, Bellows, c. 1881.
11. Minutes of Evidence, s & w bill, session 1869.
12. Notes accompanying a plan in W.R. District Offices, Gloucester.
13. Information supplied by Mr T. E. R. Morris.
14. *The Wye Tour*, 1st ed., 1818, Rev T. D. Fosbroke.
15. This bridge carried the road across the stream in the early 19th century. The stream, the Bishops Brook or Lodge Grove Brook, is known locally as 'the Shut stream' (the ironworks 'got shut of' its cinders in and around the Wye at this point) and is the county boundary with Herefordshire.
16. *The Wye and its Associations*, by Leitch Ritchie.
17. Minutes of Evidence, s & w bill, session 1869.
18. Third report of the Dean Forest Mining Commissioners, 1841.
19. *Chronology of the Tinplate Works of Great Britain*, E. H. Brooke, 1944.

Notes to Chapter 5 (*page* 64)

1. South Wales Railway Company Minute Books.
2. The Forest of Dean Central Railway, to be described in Vol. 2.
3. 30th Report of the Commissioners of Woods and Forests, 1852.
4. s & WR & C Co. Extensions and Alterations of Railway and Harbour, Etc. 1852. British Museum Map Room, Ref. MAPS 144c14.
5. s & WR & C Act, 16 & 17 Vic., c. 196.
6. More extended reference will be found in Vol. 2, under 'The Coleford Railway'.

Notes to Chapter 6 (*page* 73)

1. Minutes of Evidence, s & w bill, session 1869.
2. Ibid.
3. s & WR & C Act, 32 & 33 Vic., c. 137.
4. s & WR & C Act, 33 Vic., c. 16.
5. s & WR & C Act, 35 & 36 Vic., c. 124.
6. s & WR & C Act, 40 & 41 Vic., c. 120.

Notes to Chapter 7 (*page* 78)

1. Apparently a local term. See 'Dean Forester', 'A Note on Monmouth's stations', in *Journal of the Stephenson Locomotive Society*, June 1959.
2. To be described in Vol. 2.
3. *A Week's Holiday in the Forest of Dean*, Bellows, c. 1881.
4. Ibid.

Notes to Chapter 8 (*page* 102)

1. Much information on the various schemes for crossing the Severn will be found in *Opening of the Severn Bridge Railway*, a booklet of articles reprinted from the *Gloucester Journal* of 18 Oct 1879, also *The Engineer*, 1879, and *Engineering*, 1879.
2. sBR Act, 35 & 36 Vic., c. 109.
3. sBR Act, 40 & 41 Vic., c. 148.
4. s & w & sBR Act, 42 & 43 Vic., c. 163. The date of amalgamation, as

enacted, was that of the Board of Trade certificate authorising the opening of the SBR for passenger traffic, but the directors, in their report of 11 Feb. 1880, dated the amalgamation from 17 Oct. 1879, as do other records.

Notes to Chapter 9 (page 112)

1. GW & M (S & W & SBR) Act, 57 & 58 Vic., c. 189.

Notes to Chapter 10 (page 119)

1. In *The Practical Mechanic & Engineer's Magazine*.
2. *Two Essays in Early Locomotive History*, by C. F. Dendy Marshall, 1928.
3. *Railway Magazine*, November 1948.
4. Further particulars will be found in *Locomotives of the GWR*, Part 3, Railway Correspondence & Travel Society, 1956, which also contains a well-illustrated short account of S & W locomotives. Part 6, 1959, contains further particulars, and a line drawing, under Works No. 117.
5. These letters are preserved in B.T.C. Hist. Rec., Ref. HL/1/1/9.
6. Keeling's observations are recorded in 'The Industrial Railway Record' Nos. 3 & 4, Dec. 1963, p.58.
7. Illus. in Colburn's *Locomotive Engineering*, Vol. 2, plate 22.
8. *Contract Journal*.
9. *Engineer*, 18 June 1880.
10. *Machinery Market*.
11. Ibid. November 1881.
12. *Contract Journal*.
13. For particulars of counter-pressure braking, see *Locomotive Magazine*, 1925 & 1926, and *Railway Magazine*, June 1933.

Notes to Chapter 12 (page 145)

1. S & W deposited plan, session 1810, and Bryant's map, surveyed in 1823—1824.
2. *Hereford Journal*, 24 March 1813.
3. S & WR & C Act, 3 Geo. IV, c. 75.
4. John Murray, *Handbook for Travellers in Gloucestershire*, etc., ed. 1867.
5. E. L. Ahrons, *Locomotive & Train Working in the Latter part of the Nineteenth Century*. Vol. 4, p.58. (Reprints of Railway Magazine articles, by Heffer.)

Appendices

In the 1963 edition, we left the Severn & Wye line in a much larger, yet somewhat less hopeful, condition than it is today. The line was still in operation from Lydney Junction to Speech House Road, from Parkend to Coleford (plus the old Coleford Railway as far as Whitecliff), and from Sharpness to Berkeley Road, while the track between Lydney Junction and Sharpness, although still *in situ*, had been rendered useless by the severing of the bridge in 1960. The future for the whole system, however, was distinctly unpromising, with the possible exception of the section east of the Severn.

Today, apart from the now irrevocably isolated Berkeley Road—Sharpness section, the line has shrunk to a simple 4½ mile single track from Lydney Junction to Parkend, from whence considerable coal and ballast tonnages have been handled recently by BR. After protracted negotiations, a proposal for opencast coal working near Speech House, which would have justified retention of the line to Parkend (re-laying of the track to Speech House Road was even considered) has been rejected recently by the Government. No decision has been taken by BR regarding the future of the line, but the Dean Forest Railway Preservation Society is actively preparing to acquire it if closed, and has already re-introduced the steam locomotive into the Forest (see Appendix 2).

As to more detailed events, the latter part of 1963 saw the removal of a once familiar feature of the s & w, namely the level crossing of the South Wales line at Lydney Jcn, whilst on 12 August 1963, the main line from Coleford Jcn to Speech House Road station was closed to all traffic, although the last train actually ran on the following day, a Tuesday.

Another s & w feature was written off with the closure of Lydney locomotive shed on 29 February 1964, but a truck of coal was kept there for emergencies until diesel locomotives took over the working. On 2 November 1964 the passenger service was withdrawn between Lydney Town and Berkeley Road via the Severn Bridge. The service as between Lydney Town and Sharpness had of course ceased in 1960, due to the bridge being severed, but it had been, officially, 'suspended until further notice'. The practical effect of the closure was thus limited to the withdrawal of the auto-trains between Sharpness and Berkeley Road. On 30 November the Lydney—Berkeley Road line was formally closed for all through traffic, but the section east of the Severn remains in use for goods traffic.

The once crowded, but in later years ample, tracks in the Lydney area were greatly reduced in February 1965, when Otters Pool Jcn was taken out of use, the line thence to the engine shed lifted, and the section from Engine Shed Box to Lydney Town singled by lifting of the up main line. In February, too, the Oakwood branch was closed to traffic, being lifted in May. Some sidings in the Parkend area were also recovered, and to close a year of sombre salvage, steam operation ceased on the s & w line on and from 31 December 1965.

In May 1966 the demolition of Lydbrook viaduct was completed, not without incident as part of the approach arches collapsed without warning. The pros and cons of repairing or demolishing the Severn Bridge having been fully explored since 1960, the latter course was decided upon, and in 1967 contractors started work. The disused track between Lydney Jcn and the bridge was lifted in the period August-December, but the bridge demolition proved a considerable challenge, and was not completed until May 1970, when the last pier, No. 1, was blown.

Another cut-back to the once extensive s & w system came about on 11 August 1967, when the Coleford branch, with its extension to Whitecliff, was closed to traffic, making the short section from Parkend to Travellers Rest also redundant. Unlike the closures of earlier years, little time was lost in recovering track and demolishing station buildings, and by December 1968 nearly all of the buildings, signal-boxes and track in the Forest not in use had been removed, and lifting was in progress between Parkend and Travellers Rest.

By contrast, Parkend Goods (also known as Parkend Marsh or Parkend Wharf), which began to be used for loading opencast coal on to rail in 1961-2, has enjoyed a period of comparative boom. In December 1969 enough stone ballast and coal was being handled to justify on occasions two trains a day, and sometimes Saturday and even Sunday workings. The Sharpness branch has one booked freight service daily, mainly conveying bitumen tanks and atomic flasks.

In concluding this brief account of recent events on the Severn and Wye line, it is a great pleasure to observe that the story has not been brought to a close, whilst reminding all those who hold the remaining Forest railway dear, that its preservation into the future, beyond the needs of commercial traffic, will depend largely upon their individual efforts in supporting the society dedicated to this end.

H. W. PAAR
23 April 1972

APPENDIX 2

THE DEAN FOREST RAILWAY PRESERVATION SOCIETY

This society was formed in February 1970, with the object of purchasing, preserving and operating the remaining railway in the Forest, from Lydney to Parkend, when it is closed by BR, and to re-lay the track up to Speech House Road station site, which would provide a 5½ mile railway in a unique woodland setting, forming a valuable addition to the variety of attractions offered by the National Forest Park of Dean Forest and Wye Valley.

The society already has charge of facilities at Parkend, a Peckett 0—4—0ST, a 4-wheeled Hunslet diesel shunter, two Wickham petrol trolleys, and several goods vehicles. Further particulars may be obtained from Mr John Hancock, 'Gilnor', Worrall Hill, Lydbrook, Glos.

APPENDIX 3

LITERATURE OF THE FOREST RAILWAYS AND INDUSTRIES

When this book and its fellow *The Great Western Railway in Dean* were first published, in 1963 and 1965 respectively, there was no published work bearing on the subject, or the closely allied one of industrial history in the area, save Rev H. G. Nicholls's *The Forest of Dean* (1858) and *Iron making in the Olden Times* (1866), and widely scattered articles and references.

Although it is unlikely that the last words have been said on either subject, a major contribution has been made to that of industry in Dr C. E. Hart's *The Industrial History of Dean* (1971), which contains—inter alia— a vast amount of information on all the sites mentioned in this book, while Nicholls's two books are available again, having been reprinted in one volume in 1966. That melancholy giant, the Severn Bridge, has received attention in two articles in the *Railway Magazine*, in September 1967 and January 1970. We shall, however, shortly have a full account of the history and technology of this bridge from Mr Ronald M. Huxley.

APPENDIX 4

LOCOMOTIVES —

Number/Name	Type	Builder & Wks.	No.	Year & Gauge		
				3'—8"	7'—0¼"	4'—8½"
1.	0—4—0WT	Fletcher, J.	45	1864	—	—
2. Little John	„	„	53	1865	1869	1872
3.	„	„	54	1865	1869	1872
4.	„	„	55	1865	—	—
5. Forester	0—6—0WT	„	60	1865	1868	1872
Robin Hood	0—6—0T	„	83	—	1868	1872
Friar Tuck	„	Avonside	810	—	1870	1872
Maid Marian	„	„	940	—	—	1872
Will Scarlet	„	Fletcher, J.	122	—	—	1873
Little John	„	„	140	—	—	1874
Alan-a-Dale	„	„	157	—	—	1876
Ranger	0—6—0			—	—	
Raven	0—6—0ST	Boulton		—	—	1876
Wye	0—4—0T	Fletcher, J.	153	—	—	1876
Sharpness	0—6—0T	Vulcan	859	—	—	1880
Severn Bridge	„	„	860	—	—	1880
Sabrina	„	„	953	—	—	1882
Forester	„	„	1163	—	—	1886
Gaveller	„	„	1309	—	—	1891

BUILDING & DISPOSAL

Valuation and Allocation, 1895			Remarks	Scrapped
—	—	—	Put into dredger c.1879	
—	—	—	Withdn 1879 or 1880. Sold	
—	—	—	Withdn 1879 or 1880. Sold	
—	—	—	Sold 1872	
—	—	—	Withdn 1882. Sold	
£300	MR	No. 1121A		? 1895
£500	MR	No. 1122A No. 1605		9/1911
£860	GWR	No. 1357	Withdn 3/1910. Sold	
£200	GWR	No. 1356	Sold 11/1912. Returned to GWR 1922	1923
£1100	MR	No. 1123A		1/1905
£300	GWR	No. 1355		1/1905
£500	GWR	No. 1358	Purchased 1875. Withdn 10/1896	11/1897
—	—	—	Purchased 1879. Withdn & sold 1892	
£300	GWR	No. 1359	Purchased 1879	12/1910
£860	MR	No. 1124A No. 1606		1/1924
£1160	GWR	No. 1354		2/1906
£860	MR	No. 1125A No. 1607		8/1920
£1000	MR	No. 1126A No. 1608		12/1924
£1300	GWR	No. 1353	Withdn 10/1903	11/1903

Note.—Some of the MR locomotives were renumbered
as shown, in 1907

LOCOMOTIVES —

No./Name	Wheels Dia.	Total w/base	Cylinders Dia x Stroke		Heating Surface Total (Sq. Ft)
1, 2, 3, 4	2'—8" (1)		8"	16"	
5. Forester	3'—2"		10"	20"	
Robin Hood	4'—0"	11'—6"	14"	20"	
Friar Tuck	4'—3"	12'—6"	16"	24"	
Maid Marian (as built)	4'—0"	12'—0"	15"	22"	806
Maid Marian (as rebuilt, 1904)	4'—0"	12'—0"	15"	22"	834.12
Will Scarlet (2) (as built)	4'—0"	12'—9"	16"	24"	
Little John (as rebuilt)	4'—0"	12'—9"	16"	24"	965.8
Alan-a-Dale (3) (as rebuilt)	4'—0"	12'—9"	16½"	24"	
Wye	3'—3"	6'—0"	10"	20"	389
Sharpness (4)	4'—3"	14'—0"	16½"	24"	935.95
Ranger (as 0—6—0ST)	5'—1" (5)	13'—9"	18"	24"	

DIMENSIONS

Dia.	Boiler Length	Tubes Dia.	No.	Wkg. Press. (Lb/Sq. In.)	Weight (Total, W.O.)		Water cpty. (Galls)
2'—6"	5'—8"	1½"	60				
3'—6⅞"	8'—8½"	2"	105		28T	6Cwt	625
3'—10½"	9'—6"	2"	139	(6)	40T	2Cwt	845
4'—0"	9'—0"	2"	150	140	34T	18Cwt	800
		1¾"	193	140			
4'—0"	10'—2"	2"	151	120			980
4'—1"	9'—9½"			140	39T	10Cwt	
		1¾"	214	150	39T	18Cwt	1000
3'—1"	7'—2¼"	1½"	121	120	17T	3Cwt	330 (7)
4'—0"	9'—3"	1¾"	195	140	38T	7Cwt	932
4'—0"	11'—3"		133				

NOTES

(1) 2'—6" in the case of No. 1
(2) *Little John* and *Alan-a-Dale* had the same dimensions originally
(3) *Will Scarlet* was similarly rebuilt
(4) *Severn Bridge, Sabrina, Forester* and *Gaveller* were of the same class
(5) 4'—3" later
(6) As rebuilt by MR, 140
(7) Later 420 galls

Index

For convenience, reference to individual Acts, collieries, contractors, halts, iron mines, iron works, junctions, sidings, stations, swing bridges, tinplate works and tunnels have been grouped together under those headings.

Page numbers in heavy type denote maps or illustrations, and plate numbers are shown in heavy type at the end of each reference.